STAFFORD PAST

◆

An Illustrated History

View along Bridge Street from the roof of the Borough Free Library, 1914.

STAFFORD PAST

An Illustrated History

Roy Lewis

Phillimore

1997

Published by
PHILLIMORE & CO. LTD.
Shopwyke Manor Barn, Chichester, West Sussex

ISBN 1 86077 049 5

Printed and bound in Great Britain by
BIDDLES LTD.
Guildford, Surrey

For my wife, June

Contents

List of Illustrations

Frontispiece: Bridge Street from the Library roof

Illustration Acknowledgements

Permission to use copyright illustrations has been given by: Birmingham University Field Archaeology Unit, 3; Express and Star Ltd., 146; G.E.C. Alsthom Turbine Generators Ltd., 57, 59, 103; The General Editor of the *Victoria County History*, 93; P. Hood and the Birmingham Roman Catholic Diocesan Trustees, 142; F. Imm, 54; C.J. Lakin, 39; R.S. Rhodes, 40; Stafford Borough Council, 38, 46, 53, 61, 84, 85, 101, 102; Staffordshire Education Department, 27, 28, 44, 65, 114, 117, 125, 126; Staffordshire County Highways Department, 96; Staffordshire County Record Office, 67, 144; The Staffordshire Newsletter, 149; E. Talbot and Foxline Publishing, 31; Trustees of the British Museum, 87; the Vicar and P.C.C. of St Peter's, Rickerscote, 124.

Permission to use drawings based on 19th-century illustrations has been given by: J. Anslow, 44, 114; A.J.A. Lewis, 28, 65, 117, 125, 126.

Other illustrations are reproduced from: *The Borough Guides No. 84, Stafford* (1906), 37; J.L. Cherry, *Stafford in Olden Times*, 2, 7; A.L.P. Roxburgh, *Know Your Town: Stafford*, 25, 26, 108, 109, 113; *Stafford: an Industrial Survey* (1932), 73, 82.

All postcards are reproduced from the Lewis collection.

Introduction

When I came to live in Stafford thirty years ago I was recommended to read J.L. Cherry, *Stafford in Olden Times* (1890) and A.L.P. Roxburgh, *Know Your Town: Stafford* (1948). I found both fascinating collections of stories and information on a variety of topics, but neither was a history of the town.

In the last thirty years P. Butters, *Stafford, the Story of a Thousand Years* (1979) and the *Victoria County History* volume covering Stafford (1979) have been added to the list. The former does not live up to its title although it has very full accounts of sport and entertainment, which were the author's special interest. The latter is an invaluable reference book to which every future writer about the town will be indebted.

There is still no brief history of Stafford and in this book I have tried to fill that gap. In doing so I have drawn on all four of the books mentioned above and on many other specialist books and articles. As the book has progressed I have become increasingly aware of the need to leave out much that I would have included if space permitted.

An unexpected difficulty has been to decide the boundaries of the area covered by the book. In Saxon times the town was clearly defined by its town wall, today roadside notices tell me that I am entering (or leaving) the borough just south of Trentham Gardens. The Stafford of this book expands with time but the emphasis is on the town centre, except where a wider setting is needed.

To all who have written about Stafford in the past, to librarians, archivists, archaeologists, photographers, local historians and all those who like to talk about Stafford past, I acknowledge my debt and my gratitude. They have made the writing of this book a journey of discovery and pleasure. I hope readers will share this with me.

CHAPTER ONE

Beginnings

Stafford is almost an inland island. The town has grown up on a spit of sand and gravel between the River Sow and the Pearl Brook. Low lying marshy ground that flooded regularly lay on the banks of both rivers so that there was easy access to the site only from the north.

The marsh east of the town lies in a trough gouged out in the last Ice Age and slowly filled with mud and peat. As it silted up, pollen grains from the surrounding vegetation were trapped and their identification at different depths has built up a picture of how the environment changed.[1] Until about 5,000 years ago the area was mixed woodland. Then the tree pollen decreases, suggesting small-scale clearance of woodland and probably the first human activity in the area.

About 800 B.C. there is evidence for clearance on a larger scale—probably for farming. By Roman times pollen from cultivated plants is found, and excavation in the town in the 1980s uncovered what may have been the post holes of a Roman grain store in St Mary's Grove.[2] A minor Roman road from Blythe Bridge towards Penkridge[3] is thought to have passed across the site of Stafford and would be evidence that a ford already existed across the Sow, near the later Green Bridge. There is also some evidence of a small Roman farm near Stafford Castle. None of this suggests more than a few scattered farms in the area and these may have been abandoned in the troubled years of the Anglo-Saxon invasions.

In the eighth century St Bertelin is said to have chosen Stafford as the site of his hermitage because the place was uninhabited.

Tradition also relates that St Bertelin later moved away because the place had attracted both pilgrims and permanent settlers. The first settlement at Stafford may well date from the eighth century. Recent excavation has established the existence of a pottery industry from about A.D. 800[4] and carbon dating of wood found during excavations in St Mary's churchyard has also given a date in this century.[5]

The area was part of the kingdom of Mercia through which Danish armies marched in the late ninth century without settling. After their defeat at Tettenhall near Wolverhampton in 910, Edward the Elder, King Alfred's son, and Aethelflaed, Alfred's daughter who had the title Lady of the Mercians, fortified a series of *burhs* as bases for defence and centres where local people could trade in safety.

Stafford was fortified by Aethelflaed in 913. The defences of a burh like Stafford would be a ditch and earth bank topped by a palisade—a walled settlement not a castle. A burh was a royal town where traders were encouraged to settle and develop a market. The burgesses, as those who lived in a burh were called, made an annual payment in return for protection. The payment was divided two-thirds to the king and one-third to the Earl of Mercia, who probably had immediate responsibility for maintenance of the defences. This is the beginning of the town or borough of Stafford.

Over the next two centuries lords and churches acquired plots within the walls and settled men there. The Earl (or Lady) of Mercia probably had plots here from the time the burh was founded. The burgesses made payment to

1   Aethelflaed (Miss Nora Knight) posing with some of her Saxon retinue during the Stafford Millenary Pageant in 1913.

their lord as well as to the king. Many must have kept animals and cultivated plots of land but they were set apart from those who lived in nearby rural manors and villages because they depended upon trade, were not self-sufficient for food and, more significantly, because they were burgesses in a royal borough.

In such a varied community the need to regulate town life, ensure fair trading in the market, and settle disputes was soon obvious. The reeve, who was the king's representative in the borough became responsible for making public decisions and judgments. In time this grew into a royal court, under whose influence town life developed an ordered framework of established customs.

Stafford flourished. In the 10th century, when Edward the Elder divided the West Midlands into counties as units of royal

administration, Stafford was chosen as a county town. When, a few years later, Athelstan established a single currency for the whole kingdom, Stafford was one of the places where it was minted. The first wooden church was replaced on the same site by a stone building which can be dated to c.A.D. 1000 by coins found beneath its floor.[6] A Royal College of 13 priests under a dean was established to serve the town and neighbourhood. The pottery industry prospered. A kiln in Salter Street, dating from about A.D. 1000, can be added to the earlier kilns excavated in Clarke Street. Stafford-made pottery has been found, among other places, at Chester, Hereford and Worcester, indicating a considerable and wide-spread trade.[7] By 1066 there were 179 houses in the town with a probable population of at least 900.

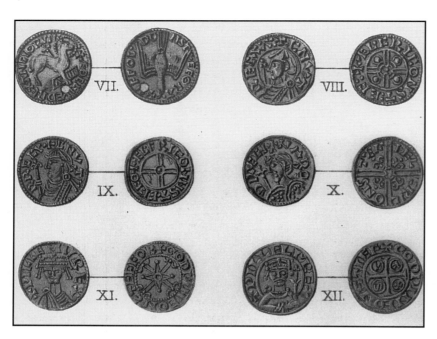

2 Coins struck at Stafford mint—VII Ethelred II; VIII and IX Canute; X Harold; XI and XII William I.

3 Bowls, cooking pots, jars and pitchers of 10th-century Stafford ware, reconstructed from sherds found near the kiln in Tipping Street.

English resistance to the Normans did not end at the Battle of Hastings. Early in 1069 a Norman army was destroyed at Durham, a combined English and Danish army captured York, and Edric the Wild led a rising of the English in Cheshire, Shropshire and Staffordshire. William with a Norman army defeated Edric's supporters at a battle near Stafford before marching north. In 1070 he was back burning crops, carrying off cattle and devastating places which had supported the rising. A number of castles were built as visible signs of Norman presence.

Stafford was the site of one of them. Its precise location is uncertain, but the medieval name Old Castle Hill for part of Broadeye probably points to its site. In order to build the castle and leave a clear space round its timber walls, 51 houses, more than a quarter of the town, had to be demolished. By 1086, when Domesday Book was compiled, the castle was no longer garrisoned but the houses had not been rebuilt.

Other changes took place soon after the Norman Conquest. King William held about half the house sites or burgages (held by the Crown before 1066) plus another 44 confiscated from the Earl of Mercia. By 1086 he had granted 54 of these to Robert of Stafford, the builder of the castle at Castlechurch, and another 39 to Roger, Earl of Shrewsbury, and his son. The king retained 48 burgages. The 14 burgages held by the Royal College at Stafford and another 14 by the Bishop of Chester were unaffected. The remaining 10 burgages were held by the abbey at Burton-on-Trent and various Norman lords. The tenants of many of the burgages held by Norman lords were attached to one of their lords' nearby manors.

For the next 250 years the population of England grew steadily, more land was cultivated, markets prospered and trade flourished. Stafford shared in this prosperity. It recovered quickly from William's destruction of part of the town and by the early 13th century the population had probably grown to at least 1,500 people.

The suburb of Foregate, north of the town, had come into being by 1170 and by 1206 those living there had acquired the same privileges as burgesses. Within the walls, excavation has shown new houses being built near Eastgate Street and other areas must have been built upon for the first time although open spaces remained. A small suburb round the Green in Forebridge, south of the town and in Lord Stafford's manor of Castlechurch, had also developed by the 13th century but its inhabitants never acquired the rights of burgesses.

By the middle of the 13th century the most vulnerable parts of the town wall had been rebuilt in stone and the three entrances to the town protected by stone gatehouses. The work probably began in 1224, when the king spent up to 20 marks on the walls and the townsmen had various taxes remitted in return for work on them. In the following years, other grants were made and in 1233 the king gave 60 oaks from Cannock Forest to make good three gaps in the remaining timber wall.[8] The North, South and East Gates were all shut at night and a watch of townsmen was posted. This was an unpopular duty and in 1307 the town was fined for failing to carry it out.[9]

A causeway carried the road from the East Gate across the Pearl Brook and the adjoining marshy land. It also dammed up the water to form the King's Pool—an addition to the town's defences. The pool provided a supply of bream, pike and tench for the king. In 1281 the queen's saucemaker was sending fish from here to the royal court in Wales.[10] In 1354 the causeway was raised to make the pool deeper and provide a head of water to power a new corn mill.

The bishop had no authority over the Royal College and its church. In the 12th century he, therefore, built St Chad's Church to provide for his tenants and be a visible reminder of his jurisdiction in the town.

The College still existed in the humble buildings and small church of St Bertelin, built several centuries earlier. At the beginning of the 13th century they began a large-scale building programme to provide a magnificent new cruciform parish church fit for a prosperous town. It was dedicated to St Mary. Building began with the nave, followed by the tower and chancel and, finally, refurbishment of the old church as a chapel. The work probably also included a new house for the dean and new quarters for the priests of the College. Traditionally King John was regarded as the patron of the new church but much of the cost must have been raised within the town from church rents. Thirteenth-century Stafford was important enough to attract the Franciscans, or Grey Friars, to the town. Their friary in Foregate had been built by 1274.

A royal court for the county, presided over by the sheriff, was sitting in the town by the 12th century and a gaol for the sheriff's use was built in 1185.[11] There must also have been a hall where the court met but there is no reference to it before 1280.

The development of local government in the town is obscure, but it is clear that the burgesses became increasingly independent while remaining under nominal royal control. In the 12th century the only officer was the reeve appointed by the king. Walter the Reeve, for example, was a wealthy man connected in some way with the household of Robert of Stafford. He had a house in the town churchyard and so was probably a burgess. He presided over the town court and was responsible for making payments from the borough to the Exchequer.[12]

In 1206 the borough received its first charter from King John. This confirmed, under royal seal, what were probably existing privileges. Burgesses were exempt from market tolls in other boroughs. Any disputes about property or debts contracted in the borough were to be settled in the borough court. The annual payment of five marks from the borough was to be accounted for in the Exchequer, not to the sheriff of the county. Further charters in 1228 and 1315 not only confirmed these privileges but also gave the burgesses the right to appoint their own coroner and build their own gaol.[13] Before the end of the 13th century the reeve was replaced by two bailiffs who were chosen annually from among the senior burgesses. This was a significant step towards autonomy.

The bailiffs presided over the town court. No records of its proceedings have survived before the late 14th century but practice probably changed little. A small court was held every two or three weeks to hear cases of debt, trespass, damage to crops, stray pigs, etc. Obviously the burgesses still had links with the land. There was no jury, but damages were assessed by two senior burgesses. A great court was held once or twice a year. There, 12 senior burgesses reported offences against the community, such as polluting wells, selling bad ale, or leaving

4 The lower courses of the medieval town wall, built into later walls, were exposed during the demolition of buildings in Mill Bank near *The Coach and Horses*.

dunghills by the roadside. Fines were levied on those responsible.[14]

The Dean and College at St Mary's claimed independence of all authority except that of the king. In the 13th century Henry III gave them the right to hold their own court and exempted their tenants from appearing in other courts for lesser offences. The dean also claimed exemption from the bishop's authority. In 1258 Bishop Meuland was refused admission to St Mary's. He then collected a mob of clerks and armed lay-men, who broke down the church doors and wounded some of the priests. In 1280 a similar attempt to gain admission by the bishop was blocked by townsmen and the sheriff. The College's independence was then confirmed by royal charter.[15]

The heart of the borough was its market. In the centre of the town an open space was paved with stones set in sand—as was the main street. Here a weekly market had been held since Saxon times. Although the townsmen cultivated plots of land and kept a few animals, the town was not self-sufficient for food. The weekly market was the means by which the town crafts-men sold their goods and local farmers disposed of surplus food in exchange. Names of burgesses suggest there were tanners, mercers, glovers, shoemakers, tailors and carpenters in the town as well as bakers, butchers and innkeepers. The pottery industry had declined but William the Potter was still supplying local needs in 1275.

In 1261 the king granted the town a six-day fair beginning on the eve of St Matthew's Day (20 September).[16] This would have attracted trade and visitors from a much wider area than the local market. Another one-day fair, on the Feast of St Peter and St Paul (29 June), was granted in 1315.

In the late 13th century, burgesses were trading in cloth at Newcastle-under-Lyme market. There was a much wider trade in wool. In 1286 the burgesses successfully claimed a monopoly of selling wool in the fleece in Stafford. In 1341 an inquiry was told that many of the better sort of townsmen 'derived their living from husbandry

5 The seal of the borough in 1583. The medieval seal was similar but had a fish below the castle instead of the fifth lion.

of wool and lambs'.[17] In the 13th century William Pickstock, one of the burgesses, was trading with Flanders and in 1332 the Subsidy Roll shows four wealthy merchants of the town probably engaged in similar trade.[18]

In the 14th century, over much of England population fell and economic activity declined. The causes are obscure, although poor harvests and plague were at least partly to blame. In Stafford the population fell sharply. Instead of being the largest town in the county, the Poll Tax of 1377 shows three other towns had become more popu-lous.[19] The decline was not reversed until the 16th century and even then the population in 1600 was probably no greater than that of 1300.

Most burgesses were in a small way of business. 'Cappers, smiths, barbers, tanners, tailors, and other handicraft men' they were called in the 15th century. There was a guild of shoe-makers, which drew up trade regulations in 1476,[20] and companies of butchers, bakers and innkeepers, which were really friendly societies providing for the welfare of their members. A trade in making woollen caps died out when the caps went out of fashion in the 16th century.

There was also a small number of richer men, mainly merchants, but including a few tradesmen in a larger way of business and perhaps the keepers of the larger inns. Best known was the Craddock family, wool and cloth merchants, who had a good London trade in the 15th century. In the next century Matthew Craddock (1520-92), a merchant of the Staple at Calais, was bailiff six times, churchwarden of St Mary's, and M.P. for Stafford.[21]

Bailiffs had to be men of standing whose decisions would be respected. By the 14th century they were chosen annually by all the burgesses but after election they consulted only a small group of senior burgesses about town affairs. In the 15th century these senior burgesses became a more formal group known as the Twenty-five. The decline of the town's trade tended to widen the gap between the Twenty-five and the rest of the burgesses and, at the end of the 15th century, with the support of the Duke of Buckingham,[22] they stopped the burgesses appointing bailiffs from outside their select group. Henceforth, the Twenty-five put forward the names of four of their number each year and the burgesses chose two of them.[23] By 1540 the burgesses were complaining that the Twenty-five had usurped all authority and were making all appointments. The burgesses then reclaimed some rights.

The borough court continued to meet, with the bailiffs presiding and a clerk to record its proceedings. Legal advice was provided by the recorder or, when the post was held by the Duke of Buckingham, by a clerk from his household. By the 15th century two chamberlains were appointed to collect fees and rents and make small payments. Most business was transacted in court but by the end of the 15th century there is some evidence that the Twenty-five occasionally met as an embryo borough council. A degree of pomp began to appear in town affairs. The bellman, who summoned the court to meet, was given a silver badge of office and two silver maces were carried in front of the bailiffs.[24]

The dissolution of the College and the confiscation of its property by Henry VIII was followed by Elizabeth's return of much of the property to the borough, which then had to pay the rector and maintain a grammar school. Additional responsibility for poor relief followed later in the century. The duties of the bailiffs were increasing steadily.

Orders regulating town life were approved by the bailiffs and the Twenty-five in 1566 and again in 1590. Richard Dorrington, the bailiff in 1591, had a copy made and presented to the town in the Black Book.[25]

The orders show the responsibility of the bailiffs for the food supply. Ale, wine and bread were to be sold at a fixed price and had to be of good quality and measure. On market days everything had to be sold in open market and it was an offence to buy more than was needed for your own household. Butchers and other sellers of food from outside the town were allowed to stand in the market but hand-made goods could only be sold there by burgesses.

Plague and disease were a constant threat. Every householder had to keep the street outside his house clean and the central drain clear so that water could run off. Those with gardens along the town ditch outside the walls had to keep it scoured to avoid stagnant water. Drinking water came from the town wells and the townspeople were forbidden to wash clothes and clean fish there, or allow horses to drink at the buckets belonging to the wells. Dung must be taken to the town dunghills outside the gates, not piled by the roadside. Pigsties had to be at least 10 feet from the street and pigs must not be allowed to run loose in the market place.

Alehouses were not to allow 'illegal games' or drinking during divine service, nor were they to harbour 'light suspect women', or allow apprentices and young people to drink after nine o'clock. Minstrels were forbidden to beg in the streets. No one was to allow persons of 'evil demeanour or unchaste living' to lodge in their house. It was an offence to park your wain where it obstructed the highway and no one was to cast stones at the doves in the churchyard. Offenders were fined from a few pence to several shillings.

6 *Above*. Thieves Ditch ran outside the town wall on the eastern side. It can still be traced by the division between the two parts of North Walls car park. This photograph shows the stone footings on which the timber defences were once raised.

7 *Right. Noah's Ark* in Crabbery Street dates back at least to the 16th century. It is said that it was built for a church dignitary before the College was dissolved and that Queen Elizabeth took wine here during her visit in 1575. This drawing shows the inn in the 19th century.

8 *Below.* Townspeople of Stafford about 1400 as depicted in the Stafford Millenary Pageant, 1913.

9 This early 19th-century print shows the High House with Shaw's House on the left; both date from the late 16th century. The black and white building on the far right, for many years known as Averill's shop, had a date 1475 on one of its beams.

The burgesses had a long-standing claim that after the harvest they could turn their animals out to graze on the open fields of Marston, north of the town. The Lord of the Manor disputed this and his objections were upheld in 1455. However, he agreed to lease Coton Field to the borough. The orders show that each year the bailiffs appointed six men to oversee the use of the field. Burgesses were allotted strips of Coton Field and, after the harvest, cattle, pigs and horses could be turned onto the stubble. Grazing on the field and on nearby marshy ground was supervised by the towns herdsman and shepherd, appointed by the bailiffs but paid by the burgesses. Every night cattle were brought back to the North Gate where their owners collected them and brought them into town for milking.

During much of the 16th century Stafford remained a town in decay. In 1540 the Act for Re-edifying Towns named it as a town where houses were out of repair. By 1570 the mill outside the East Gate was in ruins and the King's Pool reduced to a marsh. The shire hall was in such disrepair that the Assizes had been moved out of the town. In 1575, when Queen Elizabeth visited the town, she received a silver cup from the bailiffs with the words, 'Alas poor souls. Other towns give us of their wealth and you give us of your want'.[26]

In the closing years of the century there were signs of better times. The Assizes returned, bringing with them lawyers and litigants. In 1587 a new shire hall was built in the centre of the market place. The High House and other large houses in the main street were also built at this time.

CHAPTER TWO
The 17th Century

At the beginning of the 17th century evidence for what Stafford was like suddenly becomes more plentiful. There are town records, a census, and two maps. The earliest map, by John Speed, dates from about 1610. The other, from the late 1620s, survives only as a copy in the William Salt Library. These show a town still confined within its medieval walls except for the straggling suburb of Foregate and a few houses across the river in Forebridge.

A traveller from the north would enter the town between the twin towers of the North Gate. This housed the county gaol and was both insecure and laxly supervised. A woman prisoner walked out with a stolen cloak which she took to a tailor in the town to be made into breeches and another was found with a hoard of stolen property which her husband had brought into the gaol for safe keeping.[1] In 1621 a new county gaol was built a little to the east, and the North

10 John Speed's map of Stafford in 1610.

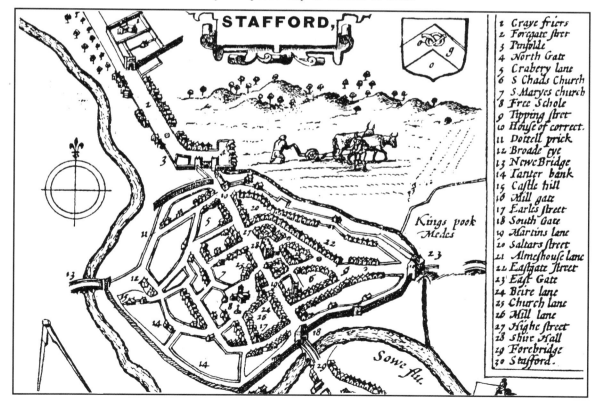

1 *Graye friers*
2 *Foregate stret*
3 *Pinfolde*
4 *North Gate*
5 *Crabery lane*
6 *S Chads Church*
7 *S Maryes church*
8 *Free Schole*
9 *Tipping stret*
10 *House of correct.*
11 *Dottell prick*
12 *Broade eye*
13 *Newe Bridge*
14 *Tanter bank*
15 *Castle hill*
16 *Mill gate*
17 *Earles stret*
18 *South Gate*
19 *Martins lane*
20 *Saltars stret*
21 *Almeshouse lane*
22 *Eastgate stret*
23 *East Gate*
24 *Brire lane*
25 *Church lane*
26 *Mill lane*
27 *Highe stret*
28 *Shire Hall*
29 *Forebridge*
30 *Stafford.*

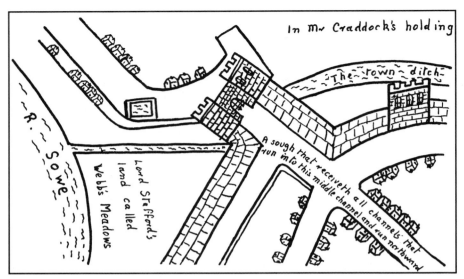

In mr Craddock's holding

The town ditch

A sough that receiveth all channels that run into this middle channel and run northward

R. Sowe

Lord Stafford's land called Webb's Meadows

11 A rough sketch taken of the North Gate and adjoining area redrawn from a copy of a 'lost' map of Stafford in the 1620s in the William Salt Library.

12 The Shire Hall built in the market place in 1586.

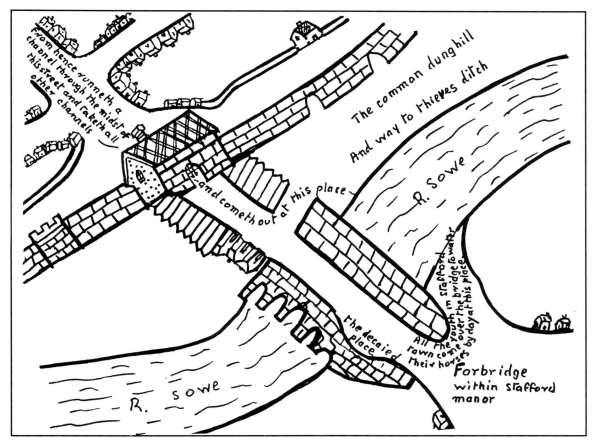

From hence runneth a channel through the midst of this street and raketh all other channels

and cometh out at this place

The common dunghill And way to thieves ditch

R. Sowe

All the youth in stafford town come over the bridge to water their horses by day at this place

the decaied place

R. sowe

Forbridge within stafford manor

13 Sketch of the Green Gate and Green Bridge redrawn from a copy of a 'lost' map of Stafford in the 1620s in the William Salt Library.

Gate became a house of correction used by the borough magistrates.

The paved main street had a central channel by which water ran off. In the middle of the town the recently built Shire Hall, 'very high and stately, with six open arches on either side and great fair pillars in the midst',[2] stood in the market place. In front of it was one of the town wells and places for the stocks and whipping post.

Continuing down the main street, the traveller would have passed a number of recently built large half-timbered houses before reaching the South, or Green, Gate and the Green Bridge over the Sow. Originally this had five arches, of which the central two were laid with wooden planks which could be taken up to make the town more defensible. In 1583 part of the town walls had been used to rebuild these arches in stone but by the late 1620s the Forebridge end of the bridge was decayed and in need of repair. The main town dunghill, just outside the walls, fouled the river here, so that horses were watered on the Forebridge side of the river, upstream from the dunghill.[3]

The walls were in very poor repair and in places no more than an earth bank and a timber stockade. A small tower near the South Gate was used as a pig sty. There was no gate house or defences at Broadeye where a 16th-century wooden bridge provided a way to Stafford Castle.

The town was small. A list of inhabitants in 1622[4] shows 385 households and a total population of 1,550, including children and 200 live-in servants and apprentices. This is small for a county town; Leicester was twice and Worcester four-times as large. Within the county, Stafford, once larger than Lichfield, was now no more than half its size, emphasising the county town's decline since the early 14th century.

There were 118 burgesses, about a third of all heads of households, most of whom were tradesmen or craftsmen but also including several butchers and alehousekeepers.[5] Most of these were in a small way of business but among them was a group of more wealthy merchants in the wool and cloth trade. Small numbers of such merchants had lived in the town since medieval times, but they seem to have been particularly prosperous in the 1590s and early 1600s, when they were building the large half-timbered houses once common in Stafford.

All of these merchants carried on a regular trade with London and, sometimes, abroad. A rare glimpse of what this meant is given by one who dashed into a council meeting 'booted and spurred' before he rode off on business. Foremost among them were the Craddocks.[6] One was a founder of the Massachusetts Bay Company, another a resident factor in Hamburg, trading with the Baltic. In Stafford the most prominent was Matthew, born in 1584, an ambitious young man with a legal training. John Dorrington had built the High House in 1595—a house fit to entertain King Charles I. His sons Francis and Richard were prominent in town affairs. Then there were Richard Drakeford, Edward Moreton, and William Moye. Moye was a mercer with a regular London trade and a son apprenticed in that city. When he died in 1636, he owned three houses in the town and land outside it. His goods were valued at £458, including plate worth £17 and a large gold signet ring.[7]

Each year on the Monday after St Luke's Day (18 October) the burgesses met to select two bailiffs and justices from four names put forward by the 21 capital burgesses. Usually one older, experienced man and one younger one were chosen. Thomas Worswick unkindly said that they chose 'a wise man and a fool.'[8] About 1610 some capital burgesses began treating other burgesses in alehouses and promising them favours if their friends were chosen as bailiffs. The wealthy merchants and professional men, like the lawyer Thomas Worswick, felt themselves threatened with exclusion from what they saw as their proper place in town affairs.

The bailiffs enforced law and order. Those who turned a blind eye to disorderly alehouses, allowed friends to brawl in the churchyard or failed to put the able-bodied poor to work spinning, brought their office into disrepute. In

14 The Elizabethan House in Gaolgate Street was built in late Tudor times, as its name suggests. It was destroyed by fire in 1887. This drawing is one of a series showing old Stafford made by H. Overton Jones of Colwich.

1612 one of the bailiffs chosen was John Towers, who boasted that he had slept with more wives than any man in town, released his friends from gaol, and kept stolen horses for his own use besides doing nothing to stop brawling and drunkenness. The more respectable burgesses had had enough.[9]

The idea of a new town charter from the king seems to have come from Thomas Craddock but most of the detail was the work of Richard Dorrington with legal advice from Thomas Worswick and enthusiastic support from Matthew Craddock, who had previously taken little part in town affairs. The aim was to ensure that only 'men of good estate of land or stock of money' became bailiffs. To that end a new body of 10 aldermen was to be nominated from the most wealthy capital burgesses. These 10 aldermen and 10 capital burgesses would form a council which would choose one of the aldermen each year as mayor, a more modern and prestigious title than bailiff. In future the ordinary, 'vulgar' burgesses would have no rôle in town affairs or elections.

Details of the new charter were kept secret from most of the burgesses until Richard Dorrington brought a draft from London for approval. Then feelings ran high. The bailiffs very reluctantly called a meeting which broke up in confusion. Opponents of the charter quickly obtained signatures of 50 burgesses on a petition against it and the bailiffs added the town seal. Meanwhile, Craddock and his friends canvassed those to be nominated as capital burgesses in the new charter until they had a majority of them in favour of it. Both opinions were sent to the king who, not surprisingly, refused to sign the charter. Its opponents rang church bells and lit a boisterous bonfire in the marketplace. However, support for the charter came from the Earls of Northampton (who was named High Steward of the town in it) and Essex. The charter was then signed by the king.

On 7 May 1614 Matthew Craddock, aged 30, was sworn in at the Shire Hall as the first mayor, while Edward Lees, insisting he was the true bailiff, marched through the market place below with his white wand of office.

Matthew Craddock kept a commonplace book for his year as mayor and from it we can learn something of a mayor's duties and of the town in the early 17th century.[10]

Stafford was a lawless town. At a single court in May 1614 the mayor as Justice of the Peace fined 22 men and two women for 17 separate cases of affray and in nine cases it is noted 'and drew blood'. At the same court 20 inhabitants were fined for 'keeping tippling houses against the statute'. Most thieves were strangers, probably beggars, found in possession of missing goods, like clothes put out to dry on hedges. The normal punishment was 'stocked and whipped' in the market place.

Any stranger passing through the town was viewed with suspicion. Henry Hewes, a Welsh weaver looking for work, and John Wood, a Lancashire man returning home after harvesting in the Vale of Evesham, were both brought before the mayor to account for themselves.

The mayor also had duties at fairs and markets. For example, at a horse fair he had to see that every sale was recorded together with the names of two vouchers as to ownership. At a market, the wardens of a town guild might seize shoes or cloth offered for sale on the grounds of poor workmanship; the mayor had to investigate.

In 1601 the Poor Relief Act ordered every parish to appoint overseers of the poor, who were to raise money by a rate levied on all householders and dispense it in the maintainance of widows, orphans and the deserving poor. Stafford appointed no poor overseers and levied no poor rate. Instead, the mayor, with some support from the churchwardens, paid out small allowances from the Corporation's income. Matthew Young, 'late prisoner of the Turks', was given 1s. as he passed through the town; Elizabeth Lucy received 6d. when her house burned down; Buller 13s. 8d. for looking after Clarke's orphan child for a year; old Widow Allaby an allowance of 5s. a quarter.[11]

The mayor paid for the Corporation's hospitality. Matthew Craddock spent 7s. 2d. on wine, sugar and cakes at the opening of the summer assizes as well as providing six gallons of wine for the judge and a gallon for the sheriff. On Easter Day he paid for 'a gallon of wine for the women'. When Lady Elizabeth's Players performed in the town he gave them 13s. 6d. and soon afterwards the Queen's Players received £1 10s.[12]

The mayor received the fines from the town courts and the tolls from the markets. Out of these he was expected to meet all outgoings. The average income was £40-£60 a year but expenses were usually at least £5 more than this.[13] This deficit was not made up by the Corporation, so that one can see why it was thought necessary for the mayor to be a man of substance.

During his year of office, Matthew Craddock paid a London goldsmith for a great gilt mace for the town.[14] He never recovered the cost. In 1617 a mayor's office was built beneath the Shire Hall to house the mace and the borough charters, in spite of protests from Francis Dorrington, one of the town chamberlains, that there was no money. When it became known that James I was to visit the town that year, Craddock and his friends were accused of trying to impress the king. Francis Dorrington suggested that they sell 'that useless gilt mace of which Craddock is so proud' in order to pay the expenses arising from the royal visit.

In preparation for the visit, the North Gate was repaired and the royal coat-of-arms painted over it. All those living on the main street were asked to paint the fronts of their houses and garnish them with flowers. James arrived by coach at the North Gate, where he mounted his horse and rode in procession to Market Square. 'The streets were glorious with the colour and joy of his visit.' After speeches and a presentation the king left by the East Gate.[15]

At times Stafford suffered from the plague. The parish registers record that Thomas Sergeant and his two sons died of it in 1593. In 1610 an outbreak closed the town's markets and led to the building of an isolated 'pest-house'. Afterwards, many of the side streets were paved and efforts made to keep the town cleaner by enforcing more rigorously bye-laws against leaving dung in front of houses. In 1631 William Waltho and his wife were prevented from entering the town because they had been in an infected house in London.[16]

At first, every mayor came from among the wealthy merchants and their friends but, by the late 1630s, such merchants were no longer living in the town. Matthew Craddock had moved to Caverswall Castle, retaining influence in the town by becoming recorder. He died in 1636. Richard Drakeford had moved to Green Hall and Francis Dorrington to London. When William Moye died, his son carried on trading from London. Richard Dorrington died leaving only a daughter who married out of town. The long line of Stafford merchants trading with London came to an end. Their places on the council were taken by local tradesmen until the Civil War disrupted life in the town.

The growing conflict between king and Parliament found most burgesses moderately royalist. They paid their Ship Money in 1635 but delayed in 1636. They sent supporters of the king to Parliament in 1640. Like many in Staffordshire they probably hoped the conflict would not affect them. It was not to be.

On 22 August 1642 Charles I raised his standard at Nottingham and the Civil War had begun. The king immediately set out on a recruiting march to Shrewsbury by way of Stafford.[17] The mayor hurriedly sent messengers as far afield as Lichfield to buy up bread to feed the king and his men. Money also had to be found for presents to those about the king, including Prince Rupert, the king's nephew and a professional soldier, who had been put in charge of his uncle's cavalry. The king stayed at the High House while men were recruited and horses requisitioned. It was from the garden there that Prince Rupert demonstrated the accuracy of the latest German pistols, with barrels that unscrewed for loading, by putting shots through the tail of

Prince *Rupert* ſtanding·in Captain *Richard Sneyd's* garden at the high-houſe there, at about 60 yards diſtance, he made a ſhot at the *weather-cock* upon the Steeple of the Collegiat Church of S. *Mary* with a ſcrew'd Horſmans piſtol, and ſingle bullet, which pierced its *taile*, the *hole* plainly appearing to all that were below: which the King then preſent judging as a Caſualty only, the Prince preſently proved the contrary by a ſecond ſhoot to the ſame effect: the two *holes* through the *weather-cocks* taile (as an ample teſtimony of the thing) remaining there to this day.

15 *Left*. Robert Plot's account of how Prince Rupert demonstrated the accuracy of the latest Continental pistols.

16 *Right*. Some of the rules for troops in the Stafford garrison drawn up by the Parliamentary Committee for the County.

All soldiers not on duty are to be ready upon the Paradoe to march to church every Sabbath day, Fast Day and Sermon Day there to hear the sermon. Whoever shall be absent shall be fined four pence to be divided in his Company.

Whosoever shall be drunk shall have nothing but bread and water for 24 hours. For a second offence to ride the horse with two flagons or pots at his back. For a third offence to be cashiered as a wicked and unserviceable man.

Whosoever shall swear shall be fined four pence for a first offence, for a second offence to ride the horse with a paper on his back declaring his offence, and for a third offence to be bored through the tongue and cashiered.

the weathercock on St Mary's Church, some 60 yards away. Old muzzle loading pistols could scarcely be relied upon to hit a man at 10 yards.

At the beginning of 1643, the king appointed Sir William Comberford as military governor of Stafford with Sir Francis Wortley's regiment quartered there for its defence. An attack by a Parliamentary rabble from North Staffordshire was beaten off and prisoners paraded in the market place.[18] In March, two Parliamentary forces under Sir John Gell and Sir William Brereton planned a joint attack on the town. When two regiments of Royalist cavalry rode into Stafford late on 18 March, they learnt that Gell was camped on Hopton Heath near the town, waiting for Brereton and his men. The next day they rode out with about a hundred infantry from the garrison and, although greatly outnumbered, charged Gell's troops with such fury that they retreated before Brereton's men could come up. The immediate threat to the town was lifted.[19]

The governor had done nothing to strengthen the dilapidated defences of the town and failed to post proper look-outs. As a result Parliamentary soldiers were able to cross the river undercover of darkness at Broadeye, where there were no defences. By morning they had secured the town and captured most of its garrison.[20]

Stafford was now a Parliamentary garrison under military rule and the headquarters of the Parliamentary Committee for the County.[21] Officially the governor worked in co-operation with the Corporation but there was no doubt as to where authority really lay. When the mayor failed to provide a rota of men to work on strengthening the defences at Broadeye, he was promptly fined £10. Captain Foxall, the only burgess among the garrison officers, was elected as an alderman and then mayor at the governor's request.

'Malignants' whose loyalty was suspect were expelled from their homes and the town. Every house was searched for arms. Soldiers were compulsorily billeted on families. A military guard was posted at each of the town gates and every night 30 townsmen patrolled the streets until 6 a.m. In addition, every family had to contribute a substantial weekly amount for the garrison's wages and the governor's expenses.

Householders were ordered to keep three months' provisions in stock in case of siege. During a scare in 1644 that Prince Rupert was about to attack the town, all the houses in Foregate and Forebridge within musket shot of the town walls were pulled down. Houses within the walls were requisitioned for those dispossessed. Land near the walls was also flooded deliberately.

Internal quarrels about the conduct of the war surfaced in December 1644 when Sir William Brereton and 300 Parliamentary troops marched into town, arrested the governor and sent him for trial in London.

The town was overcrowded with soldiers, prisoners-of-war, and townspeople—especially after houses outside the walls had been pulled down. Overcrowding led to outbreaks of fever, sickness and plague. In 1644 some prisoners were released because they were ill with fever and two years later a collection was made in London 'for distressed and infected inhabitants by the plague in the town of Stafford'.[22]

The middle years of the century saw a sharp fall in the town's population. In 1666 the Hearth Tax showed no more than 339 households, almost 50 fewer than in 1622. There was some recovery later in the century but the population never reached 1,700 and by the early 18th century was again falling.[23] During these years, mayors and aldermen were mostly drawn from better class tradesmen and shopkeepers with an occasional lawyer or other professional man. The few wealthy families in the town took little part in town affairs. There was also a substantial number of poor; 171 families were too poor to pay their Hearth Tax in 1666. When Defoe visited the town in the early 1700s he 'thought to have found something more worth going so much out of the way in it'.[24]

17 Dale's ironmongery shop in Greengate Street, on the right in this 1912 postcard, dated from the 16th century. The ground-floor shop frontage was added in 1826 but otherwise the building was little altered from Tudor times until it was pulled down in the late 1950s.

18 *Above.* This cottage was in Eastgate Street. Many similar small 17th-century houses survived in Stafford until well into the 19th century.

19 *Right.* Primrose Cottage is a small 'two-up, two-down' cottage in Mill Street. It is said to date from 1610 and was converted into a shop about 1900. This postcard shows it in 1910.

After 1650 the Corporation had an almost continuous financial crisis. Expenditure regularly exceeded income. Rents on Corporation property were raised and new burgesses charged an entry fee. Overseers were appointed to administer poor relief more strictly so that the mayor 'be not for the future troubled'. In 1671 the capital sum left by Robert Startin as a charity to provide bread for the poor was 'borrowed', with a promise that the Corporation would go on providing bread. Such short-term expedients laid up more problems for the future. Almost £600 of charity money was certainly borrowed and it has been suggested that the real figure was considerably higher.[25] In 1692 the mayor claimed that all his income except £17 had been mortgaged by his predecessor.

The Corporation's difficulties can be illustrated from the case of Coton Field. The townsmen had long standing rights in the field, which was divided into acre plots shared among the burgesses for a small annual rent. In 1653 the lease expired and the owner did not want it

renewed. Long and expensive legal arguments went on until a new agreement was reached in 1669. The Corporation had no money to pay the legal bill. They levied a contribution on all who had plots, they borrowed money against a seven-year mortgage of the market tolls and, finally, added a special supplement onto the rents of all plots for two years.[26]

Gradually, administration of the Corporation's finances became more business-like. Expenditure had to be approved by the council. After 1672, the balance on any account was carried over to the next year so that if there was a deficit the out-going mayor would be reimbursed by his successor. The town chamberlains were gradually given greater responsibility and were often appointed for two or three years together. A major reform in 1699 gave them responsibility for almost all payments, including those previously made by the mayor. However, the basic problem of insufficient income was not righted until the mid-19th century.[27]

In the years after 1660, Charles II wanted toleration for Catholics and Nonconformists but many wanted to exclude all except members of the Church of England from public life and office. The king had no legitimate children so his successor would be his brother James II, a known Catholic. The king also had an illegitimate and Protestant son, whom he had created Duke of Monmouth. Some politicians encouraged Monmouth to put himself forward as Charles' successor.

Monmouth had support among many of the townspeople in Stafford. In 1677 he was appointed High Steward of the town with his chief supporter, William Feake, as his deputy. He offended the king by a 'royal' progress through the kingdom. At Stafford, festivities were organised in his honour but Alderman Sampson Birch arranged with the king's officers to arrest Monmouth while he was in the town.[28] Afterwards, Birch accused Feake of 'proclaiming King Charles I traitor at the Market Cross in the late rebellious times'. Feake was dismissed as Deputy High Steward and a new town charter was sought, which would name new aldermen and capital burgesses. Many other towns obtained new charters about this time and they all allowed the king to remove aldermen and capital burgesses and to nominate others in their places.

By 1686 James was king and able to use his royal authority under the new charter to nominate a Catholic, Dr. Benjamin Thornborough, as alderman. In the following year, Thornborough became mayor amid scenes of near riot. In 1688 the king tried to dismiss almost half the Corporation and replace them by his nominees. The order was resisted by the Corporation and, probably, by others in the town. In October the king rescinded his order and restored the original aldermen and capital burgesses. Soon afterwards he fled overseas and ceased to rule.

Townsmen had always become burgesses in order to set up as craftsmen or traders in the town. By becoming burgesses they also gained the right to vote in the election of the town's two M.P.s. In the late 17th century this right to vote became increasingly important. William Feake was accused of 'bringing many supporters into common council' (i.e. making them burgesses) and in the 1679 election two Whig supporters of Monmouth were elected as M.P.s. They included Sir Thomas Armstrong, later executed for a plot to kidnap Charles II. In the 1680s Sampson Birch claimed that he had 'secured the admission [as burgesses] of 50 or more loyal gentlemen of worthy quality', and in 1685 two Tory M.P.s were elected to represent the town.[29]

Clearly local affairs reflected national politics, with the burgess roll being manipulated by whichever party had a majority on the corporation. Many burgesses were uncommitted to either faction and they were soon being promised rewards for their votes. Supporters also expected their loyalty to be rewarded. For a time the Chetwyns (Tory) and the Foleys (Whig) and their supporters agreed to nominate one M.P. each and so avoid a contest and limit the expense, but in 1695 Philip Foley was defeated complaining bitterly of bribery. In the early 18th century one M.P. of each party was unseated for bribery, treating, and threatening voters. Stafford elections rapidly became notorious with votes being sold to the highest bidder almost openly. This legacy of the 17th century went on until well into the 19th century.

CHAPTER THREE

Communications since 1700

In 1700 long distance traffic between London and north-west England followed the Trent Valley road via Rugeley, Colwich, Sandon, and Stone and did not pass through Stafford. This was the route followed by all London coaches until almost the end of the 18th century and this was the road taken by post-boys riding from London to Manchester and Ireland. Stafford had some importance as a centre on which local roads converged. People came to the market and fetched coal by cart and pack horse from Cannock Chase.

Roads were roughly surfaced and in winter often became almost impassable to wheeled traffic by the depth of mud and deepness of ruts. By the 1760s canals were being constructed to carry heavy and bulky freight more cheaply than by road. In the Midlands the Trent and Mersey Canal followed the Trent Valley and brought prosperity to Stone where the company had its head office. The Staffordshire and Worcestershire Canal was built to link the River Severn with the Trent and Mersey Canal at Great Haywood. Neither canal passed through Stafford.

The nearest point of the canals to Stafford was at Radford where the Staffordshire and Worcestershire Canal passed under the road to Lichfield. Here the canal company built a wharf and warehouse where freight for Stafford could

20   Radford in 1926. Since then the *Trumpet Inn*, on the right, has been rebuilt further back from the road and more recently renamed *The Radford*.

Railway, Weighing Machine, Canal Boats, &c.

TO BE SOLD BY AUCTION,

By HENSHAW AND SMITH,

At the Star Inn, in Stafford, on Friday the 15th day of July, 1814, at 5 o'clock in the afternoon,

THE undermentioned Property, viz:—The Railway and Sills between Stafford and Radford, being about a mile and a half in length, laid with Flanch Rails; a capital Weighing Machine, capable of weighing 5 tons, with machine house and blacksmiths shop at the Green, in Stafford; 2 Canal Boats; 2 short River Boats; a quantity of Railway Carriages capable of carrying from 20 to 30 cwt each; a Crane with wheels, &c. and sundry other articles.

For particulars or to view the Railway, &c. apply to Mr. JOHN BARKER, of Radford Wharf, near Stafford. 17th June, 1814.

21   The sale of tramway equipment advertised in the *Staffordshire Advertiser*, 2 July 1814.

be unloaded to await collection by cart. No improvement was made for over 30 years until in 1805 the Stafford Railway Coal & Lime Company was formed to construct a tramway on which horse-drawn wagons could be hauled from Radford to Stafford. It started alongside a basin behind the Radford warehouse and ran by the side of the Lichfield Road to near the Green Bridge. Each wagon carried 30 cwt. of coal or lime. The venture was not a success and closed in 1814.[1] Wooden sleepers from the tramway were dug up on the south side of Lichfield Road in 1880 and sandstone blocks from the basin were found when Radford Marina was extended in 1972.

A better solution replaced the tramway. A lock was constructed to allow boats to pass from the canal to the River Sow which was deepened and straightened for the 1½ miles into Stafford.

For the last 200 yards before the Green Bridge a canal was cut parallel to the river. Here there was a coal wharf reached from Bridge Street. The work was financed by South Staffordshire coalmasters and leased to The Gornall Colliery Company until 1838 when the lease was bought by the canal company for £50.[2] In the late 19th century William Moss, builder, railway contractor, and coal merchant occupied the wharf. By 1930 it was disused and soon afterwards the short canal by the Green Bridge was filled in.

As the industrial output of the Black Country rose, the road from Wolverhampton through Stafford to Stone and the north became increasingly busy. Late in the 18th century, the growth of Stafford itself and its shoe manufacture added to the traffic on the roads to both Stone and Lichfield and thence to Manchester or London. Stafford gained a new importance as a road centre.

22 These houses on the Lichfield Road are set back with a wide pavement in front along which the tramway rails were once laid. Alterations were made when the Queensway traffic island was built in the 1970s.

23 The River Sow east of the Green Bridge with the canal and coal wharf on the left, parallel to the river on the right.

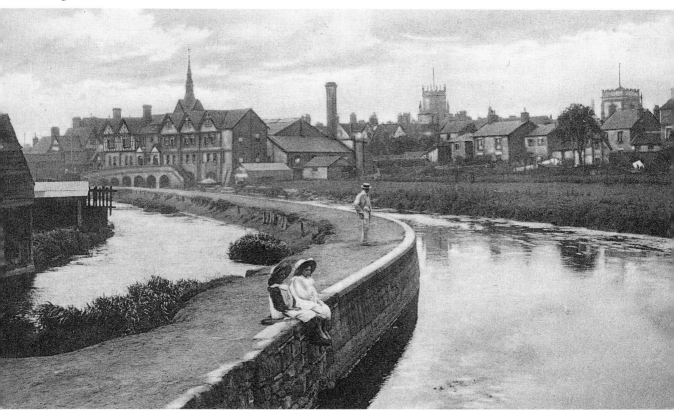

Tolls.   For every Horfe, Mare, and Gelding, Mule, or other Beaft (except an Afs) drawing in any Carriage, the Sum of Sixpence :
   For every Horfe, Mare, Gelding, Mule or other Beaft (except an Afs) laden or unladen and not drawing, the Sum of Two-pence :
   For every Afs when drawing any Carriage the Sum of Three-pence ; and when not drawing any fuch Carriage, the Sum of One Penny :
   For every Drove of Oxen, Cows, or Neat Cattle, the Sum of One Shilling and Eight-pence *per* Score, and fo in Proportion for any greater or lefs Number : And,
   For every Drove of Calves, Swine, Sheep, or Lambs, the Sum of Tenpence *per* Score, and fo in Proportion for any greater or lefs Number :
   And on every *Sunday* (to be computed from Twelve of the Clock in the preceding *Saturday* Night, to Twelve of the Clock in the next fucceeding Night) Double the Tolls which fhall for the Time being be authorized to be collected on any other Day under or by virtue of this Act :

24 *Left.* A list of tolls charged on the roads from Stafford to Uttoxeter and Newport from the Act of Parliament renewing the turnpike trust in 1814.

25 *Right.* The turnpike toll house at the junction of the Weston and Tixall roads. The site is now occupied by *The Gate* public house.

During the 18th century a determined effort was made to improve the main roads. Instead of unpaid amateur surveyors appointed by each parish through which a road passed, turnpike trusts were formed. These raised capital and appointed paid surveyors to maintain and improve a road, the cost being recouped by charging all who travelled on it. As the roads improved the traffic on them increased.

The main Trent Valley road had been turnpiked before 1730 but it was not until 1761 that the road from Wolverhampton through Stafford to Stone was taken over by a trust and toll gates placed across it at Rising Brook and on the northern outskirts of Stafford. In 1763 another trust took over the roads from Stafford to Sandon and Eccleshall while the roads to Newport, Uttoxeter and Cannock were not turnpiked until 1793.[3] Besides smoother and more hard wearing road surfaces the trusts also improved the line of many roads. An example is the present Newport Road which, until 1793, ran along what is now Rowley Avenue, Hargreaves Lane, and an old hollow way still traceable to the east of Castle Bank.[4]

Traffic through the town had to pass under the narrow North and Green Gates at each end of the main street and across an almost equally narrow Green Bridge. The Green Gate was demolished in 1777 and Green Bridge rebuilt as a single span brick and stone arch in 1781.[5] Richard Whitworth, who owned property at the end of the bridge, claimed it had been done on his initiative to provide 'a noble opening at the entrance of the town'. During the Napoleonic Wars he turned his property into a martello tower with swivel guns to defend the town in case of a French invasion.[6] When the North Gate was demolished in the 1790s the last obstacle to traffic was removed.

By the 1770s gentlemen's coaches were appearing on the streets of Stafford and four-wheeled chaises were available for hire in the town. In 1785 the main post-road from London to Manchester and Ireland was diverted through Stafford and mail coaches were introduced instead of post-boys. Stage coaches from London to Manchester, Liverpool and Chester, now passed through the town, as well as coaches from Birmingham and Wolverhampton to the north-west. For a time in the 1780s there was even a coach from Bath to Manchester via Stafford.[7]

The Star, *The George*, *The Dolphin*, *The Swan* and *The White Bear* along the town's main street were refurbished to provide accommodation for travellers and often yards where coaches could stop to change horses, and passengers could snatch a quick meal. The larger inns had stabling for considerable numbers of horses and owned fields where they could be turned out. In 1805 a recently renovated *Swan Inn* had stabling for 50 horses and the proprietor leased 70 acres of pasture and meadow near the town.[8]

By the early 19th century Stafford was the place where busy roads from London and Wolverhampton came together on the way to Manchester and the north-west. Twenty-four coaches passed through every day. National carriers like Pickford & Co. and Thomas Ashmore had depots in the town. In addition, there was a regular service of wagons travelling to Gnosall, Newport, Penkridge, Wolverhampton, Stone, Newcastle, Uttoxeter, Derby, Manchester and Rugeley.[9]

Roads had improved so much that stage coaches were reaching what were then considered to be high speeds. *The Hark Forward* left the *Star Inn* in Stafford at 10 a.m., reached Wolverhampton at 12 o'clock and Birmingham at 2 p.m.[10] Allowing for time taken changing horses, this gives a speed of about 10 m.p.h. It is not surprising that coaches were given names like *The Rocket*.

This was to come to a sudden end. In 1832 the merchants of Manchester and Liverpool already saw railways as the transport of the future and were planning the first trunk line to link their towns with Birmingham. The route chosen was largely through open countryside, passing through only one town north of Wolverhampton. That was Stafford. A station and approach road were built just outside the town and to the north of Newport Road. To the south of the station, the line had to cross 'a rotten bog'. Several

26 A 19th-century print of *The Swan Inn*, the main coaching inn of the town. The archway led through to a yard where the coaches stopped to change horses. The stables were behind the yard.

thousand cubic yards of material sank before the line was finally laid on brushwood over-topped by thick layers of sand and ashes.[11]

The line was formally opened on 4 July 1837. The Grand Junction Railway Company, as it was called, organised no official celebration because the country was in mourning for King William IV who had died a few days earlier. However, the Mayor of Stafford ordered a small field-piece to be fired to salute the arrival and departure of the first train into the station. The Union Jack was flown and large crowds lined both sides of the line.[12]

There were six trains daily in each direction; the fare from Stafford to Birmingham was four shillings (20 pence).[13] Speeds of over 25 m.p.h. were reached. A passenger wrote from Stafford,

We came from Birmingham here, 30 miles, in an hour and five minutes and from Wolver-hampton, 16 miles, in 28 minutes. You see but little of the country by reason of the rapidity. It is in vain to try and catch the features of a person you pass.[14]

The claret-coloured first-class carriages each had a name like a coach and each compartment was fitted with six seats as coaches had been. First-class seats were numbered and tickets sold with corresponding numbers.[15]

Once the railway was open, stage coaches could not match its speed and comfort. A traveller from Stafford wrote, 'No one having once travelled by it would ever trouble horses again if he could avoid it'.[16] From the opening day mail transport had been transferred to the railway. Long-distance coaches ceased to run and coaches were limited to short journeys to collect passengers and deliver them to the nearest rail-way station.[17] The coming of the railway was a disaster for coach proprietors and those innkeepers who had relied on coach passengers for much of their trade. Dickens, visiting Stafford a few years later, described *The Swan* as 'the extinct town inn, the Dodo, in the dull High Street'.[18]

London-bound travellers on the Grand Junction Railway had to change trains at Birmingham. A line from Stafford via Tamworth

---

OPENING OF THE GRAND JUNCTION RAILWAY

Many, if not all, of the Coaches between Birmingham and Liverpool and Manchester will be taken off the roads ; but, it is probable that a number of branch Coaches from places east and west of the line to the different stations will be started. One is advertised to run daily between Uttoxeter and Stafford : and an omnibus daily between the Potteries and Stafford. A coach will be put on the road between Lichfield and Stafford ; and one will start on Tuesday from Shrewsbury through Drayton to Whitmore. The Potteries will, of course, have means of conveyance to the nearest point of the Railway, for passengers to Liverpool and the North.

ON Tuesday next, an OMNIBUS will start between the STAFFORDSHIRE POTTERIES and STAFFORD, to run daily; entitled
THE NOVELTY;
To start from the Bull's Head, Burslem, every morning at seven o'clock, and to arrive at the Swan Hotel, Stafford, in time for the First Class Train of Steam Carriages : to leave Stafford at half-past six o'clock, and arrive at Burslem at half-past eight.

JOHN MEESON, STAFFORD.
WM. MEESON, STONE,
ED. NICHOLLS, BURSLEM.

27 Report and advertisement in the *Staffordshire Advertiser*, 1 July 1837, showing the effect of the opening of the Grand Junction Railway on coach traffic through Stafford.

28   The railway station in 1844 after the first station had been rebuilt.

and Rugby would not only avoid the change but also shorten the journey by 50 miles. Plans for such a Trent Valley Railway had been drawn up as early as 1836 but construction was delayed by difficulties in negotiating terms for crossing the Shugborough estate. The Trent Valley line from Stafford to London was not officially opened until 26 July 1847. The first train left Stafford station with church bells ringing and coloured streamers suspended across the line. Even before the line opened, the Grand Junction, the Trent Valley and the London to Birmingham Railway Companies had amalgamated to form the London North Western Railway Company.

Stafford had become a busy railway junction. The original station had had to be replaced by a larger one in 1843-4. Refreshment and dining rooms were added five years later, but this station too would soon be outgrown.

In 1849 the Shropshire Union Railway & Canal Company built a line from Stafford to Shrewsbury which was immediately leased to the LNWR and became a busy linking line as that company extended its operations into Wales.[19] In

1860 the LNWR made Stafford the point where their north and south divisions met and trains were handed over to new drivers and different locomotives. New engine sheds were built to house 37 locomotives and a new suburb, Castletown, grew up near the station to provide homes for railway workers and their families. By 1862, 450 tickets a day were being sold at Stafford station.[20]

In 1862 the old station was demolished and a new one built in what was described as an Italian style. In 1866 Victoria Road was laid out to provide a direct approach from the town to the station, with a new bridge over the River Sow. *The North Western Hotel*, facing the station, was opened in the same year by Mr. Wood, late of *The Swan Inn*. The new hotel had a coffee room and private sitting rooms for ladies as well as bars, a smoking room and a billiard room for gentlemen.[21]

In 1862 a railway from Stafford to Uttoxeter, with links to Derby and Ashbourne, was authorised against fierce opposition from the LNWR who objected to the new railway having the right to

29 *Above*. The exterior of the railway station remained substantially unchanged from 1862 to 1963. This postcard shows the station and the *Station Hotel* in the 1920s.

30 *Left*. Stafford Common station in the 1950s.

31 The level crossing at Queensville before a road bridge was built over the railway in 1898. The view was taken looking towards Stafford.

run into Stafford station. The line opened in December 1867 with the LNWR being deliberately obstructive. It was said to be easier to reach the Continent than to travel by rail to Uttoxeter via Stafford. A station at Stafford Common was opened in 1874 and in 1881 the Great Northern Railway took over the line. A new platform for Uttoxeter trains was built at Stafford station and Stafford Common station was rebuilt. After that relations between the two companies improved, although the GNR had its own station-master and staff at Stafford until 1915.[22]

Until the growth of road transport, every commodity from perishable milk, meat and fish to coal and minerals was carried by rail. Every village and town depended upon supplies brought by rail. Goods traffic was organised by wagons which were assembled into trains, detached, shunted and remarshalled into new trains. Stafford

was the point to which wagons from Wales, Manchester, Birmingham, London, Nottingham, and even those with Burton beer were brought to be sorted according to the destination of their loads. The extensive freight marshalling yard with its own locomotives added to the importance of Stafford as a railway centre.[23]

During the First World War the railways came under government control and after the war were formed into four regional companies of which the London, Midland and Scottish Railway operated all lines through Stafford except the line to Uttoxeter. The companies failed to adapt to the rapid growth of bus services, road haulage and travel by motor car. In 1939 they were again taken into government control and, later, nationalised by the Transport Act (1947). It was not until 1955 that plans were made to slim down and modernise railway services.

32   No. 1 platform on Stafford station in 1907 with a typical L.N.W.R. sign giving the time of the next train to London.

Around Stafford, the Uttoxeter line beyond Stafford Common station and Royal Air Force No. 16 Maintenance Unit. (Stafford) had been closed to passengers in 1939. Freight traffic was reduced after the war, but complete closure of the line was delayed until 1975 when the Maintenance Unit switched to road transport. The Shrewsbury line closed in the 1960s. Changing patterns of working meant that locomotives were no longer kept at Stafford and the locomotive sheds closed in 1965.

Only the old Grand Junction and Trent Valley lines remained open. These were modernised and made more attractive to passengers and freight. Electrification of the main line between London and Manchester was completed in 1967, giving a faster passenger service. A new signalling system with fewer boxes was introduced. Stafford station was entirely rebuilt and given new refreshment rooms and a mechanised booking office in 1963.[24] Today, Stafford remains an important railway junction and a future stopping place for Channel Tunnel trains.

At the beginning of the 20th century roads were suffering from years of neglect. All the turnpike trusts round Stafford had amalgamated in 1867, and were abolished in 1880 when the toll gates were removed. At that time traffic on the roads was limited to local delivery carts, a few private carriages, and horse-drawn wagons going to and from villages on market days. The first vehicles powered by internal combustion engines appeared in the late 1880s and in 1903 they were required to be registered and assigned number plates. There were then 18,000 such vehicles in the whole of Great Britain. In Stafford, the Stafford Motor Services & Supply Company started a motor bus service from Radford to Stafford Common in 1907 but it was short lived because the vehicles were unreliable.[25] Postcards of the town's main street show how few motor vehicles were to be seen before 1920.

33 This Panhard Levassor is said to have been the first car from Stafford registered under The Motor Car Act of 1903, which introduced number plates.

34 Martin Mitchell's Stafford Motor Service & Supply Co., began a regular motor bus service from Radford to Stafford Common in November 1907 using an open-topped double-decker bus. The service was immediately popular and this bus was added to the service in January 1908.

35 A postcard view of Gaolgate, *c*.1910. The only motor car to be seen is parked in the distance near The High House.

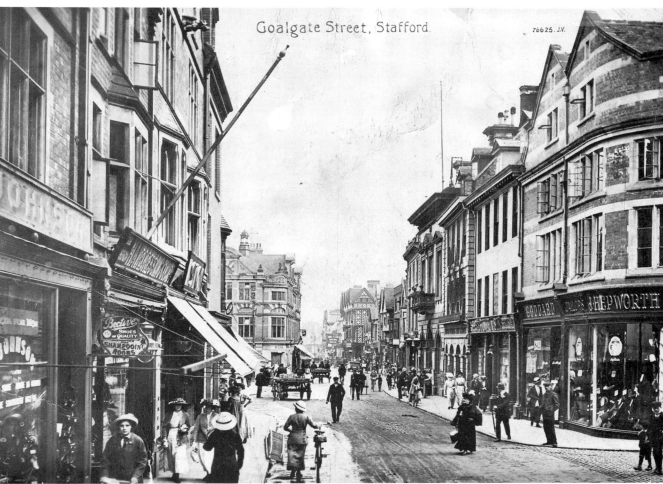

After 1920 change was rapid. By 1922 both the Birmingham Midland Motor Omnibus Company and the Potteries Electric Traction Company had motor-bus garages in the town and their services spread in direct competition with the railway. Road haulage, with the advantage of door-to-door delivery, spread even more rapidly. All the traffic from Stoke-on-Trent and Manchester to the Black Country and beyond had to pass along the main street of Stafford.

By the 1930s the town was becoming well known for its traffic congestion. In 1934 the Jubilee Fountain in Market Square was demolished to make way for the town's first car park. The Borough Council began a piecemeal attempt to widen Gaolgate. Discussions took place about a by-pass, but shopkeepers were opposed as they feared loss of trade. A census in 1938 measured the traffic passing along the main street as over 13,000 tons a day. Early in the Second World

36 An advertisement for Boxall's Garage in 1932, showing a typical family car of the period.

GO TO

BOXALL'S GARAGE
LICHFIELD ROAD, STAFFORD

for
Demon-
strations
and
Advice

for
Sales,
Part
Exchange
and
Deferred
Terms

and for Real After-Sales Service

on "TRIUMPH" CARS

Tel. No. 397   Sole Agents for Stafford and District

37 Bailey's Motor Garage in Lichfield Road (opposite the Malt and Hops) in 1906, with vehicles posed outside.

38   Greengate Street in 1946, showing the congestion caused by heavy goods traffic.

War a Defence Regulation banned all parking in the main street to ease the flow of essential goods through the town.[26]

In 1948 the Borough Surveyor produced a report on future developments entitled *Stafford Survey*. This suggested an outer ring road, which included Beaconside and the proposed national motorway (M6), an intermediate ring of improved existing roads and an inner ring road. The eastern part of the inner road was to be a new road from Gaol Square to Lichfield Road across land where there were only a few outworn cottages and some commercial property. This would allow through traffic to be banned from the main street. The suggested inner and outer ring roads have been the starting point for most subsequent planning.

The Borough Council's deputation to the Ministry of Transport to discuss an inner ring road in 1951 were told that priority must be given to the motorway by-pass round the town. Planning for this began in 1955 and construction four years later. The County Council were in charge of the project with John Laing Construction and J.L. Keir the main contractors. At one time 500 men were working on the site and living with their families in caravan camps. The six-mile length of motorway was opened on 2 August 1962 by Ernest Marples, Minister of Transport, who announced, 'the end of Stafford's black reputation as one of the most congested towns in the country'.[27]

It was soon clear that he had been over optimistic. Discussions between the Borough

39 *Left*. The traffic island under construction at the Lichfield Road end of Queensway. The wall in the centre is part of the Forebridge lock-up and the garage on the right is the successor to Bailey's garage (illustration 37).

40 *Right*. Construction of Queensway near Lammascote, showing the reinforced concrete deck in the foreground. In the background, piles that have already been sunk are being tested.

Council and the Ministry of Transport about an inner ring road were resumed in 1965 and detailed design work on the new road from Gaol Square via Lammascote to the Lichfield Road at White Lion Street began in 1970. Local Government re-organisation in 1974 transferred responsibility to the County Council, who reduced costs by abandoning pedestrian subways and fly-over junctions in favour of traffic islands and traffic lights. Much of the road was to be built over marsh where wet peat and silt lay to a depth of over 50 feet. Five hundred and fifty piles had to be driven down to the Keuper marl below the silt as a foundation.

The new road, named Queensway, was opened on 12 June 1978. Its traffic lights quickly became notorious. A newspaper correspondent a week after the opening wrote, 'We took the kids to ride round Queensway ... we liked the road; it will save a trip to Blackpool lights this year.'[28]

The opening of Queensway has allowed traffic to be banned from the main street. The inner ring road now extends to Broadeye and existing roads have been improved to complete the circle. Building an outer ring road to the east of the town is still the subject of fierce controversy with every suggested route being unacceptable.

CHAPTER FOUR

Industry since 1700

Stafford in 1700 was still a small market town. Self-employed craftsmen worked there and sold from their homes. No one was allowed to set up in business unless he had first become a burgess and paid a stiff £10 admission fee.[1] Their customers were townspeople and those who came from nearby villages on market days.

In practice, unauthorised tradesmen were common, at least from the 1650s. By the late 17th century, outsiders wishing to practise their craft in the town were often given a licence, which did not give them a vote at election time, rather than being admitted as burgesses.[2] During the early 18th century, as the number of licence-holders grew, restrictions on setting up in business broke down.

The town had a tradition of shoemaking. There had been a shoemakers' guild as early as 1476 and in the early 17th century its wardens were still inspecting shoes displayed for sale in the market place. Some shoemakers lived in cottages and made a bare living. Others were moderately prosperous. None was wealthy. When John Godwyn died in 1708 he had in his workshop five calf skins, three hides and butts, two kips (skins from one-year-old cattle), four dozen heels, 15 pairs of men's shoes, 20 pairs of women's shoes, 20 pairs of children's shoes and two pairs of boots.[3] He probably employed a live-in apprentice and one or two journeymen who worked in a room next to the street with finished shoes displayed on a trestle outside.

The first to manufacture shoes on a larger scale was William Horton, the eldest son of Walter Horton, a shoemaker in the town.[4]

William had been born at Stafford in January 1750 and is said to have set himself up in business when he was only 17 years of age. By the late 1770s he had introduced a system of outworkers like that found in other shoe-manufacturing towns. Leather for the uppers and soles of shoes was cut out in his workshop. (This was to become a specialist trade known as clicking.) The pieces were then given to outworkers, who made up shoes in their own homes and returned them to Horton's warehouse, where they were inspected and the workmen paid and given leather for another week's work.

41   William Horton (1750-1832).

The system presupposed a market for mass produced shoes. By the late 18th century this existed in London, new industrial centres like Birmingham and Manchester, and colonies abroad. By 1785 Horton was buying skins from as far away as Ireland and selling his shoes to a London factor, Thomas Bell, by whom many were exported. When Horton could not find enough outworkers he

> employed 50 or 60 day labourers who have learnt the manufacture in the course of a year. They can get their living from the first week they begin to learn, and those same men in a very little time have taken apprentices themselves and taught others the business.[5]

During the Napoleonic wars in the 1790s, Bell became the government agent for procuring shoes for the army and was buying £1,000-worth of shoes at a time from Horton, clearing all his stock and that of other manufacturers in the town. By 1813 Horton had his own warehouses in Manchester and Liverpool and was exporting large quantities of shoes to America. He also opened a shop for better quality shoes not far from St Paul's Cathedral, but this was not a success.

The scale of Horton's enterprise was immense for its day. In the early 1800s he employed nearly 1,000 outworkers in and near Stafford. His annual turnover was almost £75,000 and his profits large enough for him to lease Chetwynd House, the town house of the Chetwynd family, in Greengate Street and to build new workshops and a warehouse behind it. He became the dominant figure in local society.

Other shoe manufacturers followed Horton's example, but never on the same scale. Bailey's *British Directory* in 1784 names William Allenranthaw, Francis Brat, George Godwin, Thomas Kingston, and William & John Taylor. By 1793 the number of shoe manufacturers had risen to thirteen.[6] Some of them must have been manufacturing on a small scale since the population of the town was still below 4,000.

By 1812 the industry had become depressed. Trade with America had been disrupted by war; the government had imposed an additional tax on leather; and competition from Northampton, where wages were lower, was fierce. Army contracts had been lost. Horton reduced his outworkers to about 400 and was said to have stock worth £25,000 in his warehouse with two or three men employed to clean the shoes and stop them rotting. His business never recovered and he seems to have retired before he died in 1832.

Trade did revive in the 1820s with more women's shoes being made and new names among the manufacturers. Notable among these was Thomas Bostock, the son of a Derbyshire cordwainer, who started making boots and shoes in Gaolgate about 1820. By 1834 he employed 200 men and was the largest shoe manufacturer in the town. He later moved his premises to a site in Foregate, next to the Infirmary, with his son Edwin as his partner.[7] By 1836 the mayor could claim that Stafford carried the largest trade in women's shoes of any town in the kingdom.

Among outworkers, sewing thin leather uppers was usually work for women or boys, while the heavier sowing of thick soles to uppers was men's work. By 1855 a sewing machine capable of sewing thin leather had been developed in the U.S.A. At that time trade was flourishing with new markets opening in Australia where the gold rush had led to a rapid rise in population. In order to increase production, Edwin Bostock imported three of the American machines and set them up in his Foregate works.

Men from every manufactory in the town held a mass protest in Market Square. They declared that the new machines would put women out of work and so reduce their families to poverty. They would not work on machine-sewn tops and formed a union to concert action. The machines were withdrawn.[8]

The Stafford manufacturers quickly lost trade to those places which had accepted the sewing machine. In 1858 they formed an Association and announced that sewing machines would be introduced. In March 1859 all their men came out on strike and remained out until July, when hardship forced them to agree to work on machine-sewn tops.[9]

42 Factory with women working on shoe uppers. The photograph was probably taken at Lotus Ltd. in the early 1930s.

43 The Stafford Trades and Friendly Societies Infirmary Procession in 1906. A visiting delegation from Northampton parades with the branch banner of the Union of Boot and Shoe Operatives. A collecting sock for coins is suspended below the banner.

The introduction of machines was also the introduction of factories. Instead of working at home, women now had regular factory hours. Manufacturers claimed that working conditions were healthier and homes tidier. By 1862 Bostocks had opened a factory for 200 women aged 12 and upwards who worked from 8 a.m. to 7 p.m.[10] The heavier work of sewing on soles was still done by male outworkers.

In the 1870s the Blake Sole Sewing Machine was gradually introduced. Over the next 20 years this was followed by other machines to fit eyelets, to rivet heels, etc. Making shoes became a factory industry with many specialist trades. In 1874 the men, who had been members of the Amalgamated Society of Cordwainers, a craft society, decided to break away. At a meeting in Stafford in February 1874, the National Society of Boot and Shoe Riveters and Finishers was formed for factory workers.[11]

Land north of the town had become available for building after the enclosure of Foregate Field in 1807. When the shoe industry revived and the town's population rose in the 1830s, houses for the growing number of outworkers were built there. After the mechanisation of the industry, the population grew even more rapidly—from 10,472 in 1851 to 19,977 in 1881. Many of the additional houses, and almost all the new shoe factories, were built in Foregate which became a suburb of shoe workers.

The first factories were small two- or three-storeyed buildings employing only a small number of people. Frederick Riley's factory was typical.[12]

Most of the factories were started by men of humble origin like David Hollin, the son of a railway guard who had settled in one of the terrace houses of Castletown.[13] He worked as a clicker at Bostocks until he secured financial backing from Zachariah Anderson, Secretary of the Old Stafford Building Society, and set up in business for himself in Horton's old premises behind Chetwynd House. In 1873 he moved to a newly-built factory on the corner of Rowley Street and Marsh Street, laid out to his own specification. The business flourished and Hollin grew rich. He built Highfield Manor on Newport Road as a home for himself, his wife and his niece.

44 *Above*. Frederick Riley began manufacturing shoes with five employees in this factory behind Bigham & Son's shop in Gaol Square in 1880.

45 *Left*. David Hollin with his wife and niece about to drive away from his home at Highfield Manor on Newport Road. The coachman's lodge and gate posts to the Manor still exist at the lower end of High Park.

46 *Right*. An aerial view
showing the Sandon Road
factory of Lotus Ltd. about
1948.

47 *Below*. The clicking room
at Bostock's factory in 1907.
Clickers laid out patterns for
the uppers of shoes and cut
out the various pieces.

By 1900 the increasing use of specialist
machines was leading to fewer but larger
factories. The number decreased from 39 in 1880
to nine in the 1930s while the number of
workers in the shoe industry remained almost
constant at just under three thousand. When
Bostock's factory in Foregate burned down in
1901 it was replaced by new and larger premises
on the Sandon Road. J.J. Heys, who had

emigrated from Stafford to America, was brought
back to introduce the latest American ideas in
production and technology.[14] By this time the
company, like most other Stafford manufacturers,
was specialising in women's shoes. The factory
has been extended several times and in 1919
the company was enlarged by amalgamation with
Frederick Bostock Ltd. of Northampton and
renamed Lotus Ltd.

Lotus Ltd. came to dominate the town's shoe industry. By the 1930s it employed more than half of all the shoe workers in the town. Much of the new machinery installed at this time was leased from the British United Shoe Machinery Company, who serviced the machines and supplied spare parts from their depot in Stafford.[15] After the Second World War competition from cheap foreign shoes grew. In 1950 the five manufacturers in the town were producing 20,000 pairs of women's shoes a year. By the 1970s Lotus was the only shoe manufacturer in the town. By 1995 the number of workers had fallen to 600 and in the following year the Fii Group, who had taken over the company, transferred half of these jobs to a new factory outside the town.[16]

The only other shoe company to survive today began in the 1860s as R.J. Jennings & Son. Soon after 1900 they gave up making shoes to become wholesale distributors. In 1959 the name was changed to Jen Shoes Ltd. At that time the

company was distributing over one million pairs of shoes a year. They had also become suppliers of special footwear to expeditions to the Himalayas and elsewhere.[17]

The flourishing 19th-century shoe industry attracted a number of specialist businesses to the town. As the industry changed and the number of manufacturers fell, some of these closed and others diversified into new products. John & William Keats (later Keats & Bexon) manufactured shoe machinery in Gaol Road from the 1870s until they closed in 1967.[18] John Evans began making knives for the shoe industry in Fancy Walk about 1880. After several changes of name the company is now J.H. Lines Ltd., making a variety of tools at a factory on the Stone Road.[19] Shoe Findings began as a maker of cardboard boxes for shoes. Since 1945 it has become The Stafford Box Co. and expanded into other types of packaging.[20] About 1920 Heels Ltd. built a factory in Friars Terrace to make wooden heels. They became the largest manufacturer in the

48   Aerial view of Heels of Stafford's factory in Friars Terrace in the 1930s. Friars Cottage is to the right of the factory.

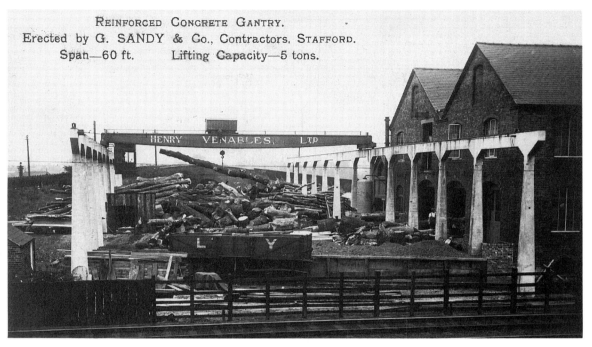

REINFORCED CONCRETE GANTRY.
Erected by G. SANDY & Co., Contractors, STAFFORD.
Span—60 ft.   Lifting Capacity—5 tons.

HENRY VENABLES, LTD.

49   Henry Venables Ltd., showing the gantry erected in 1920 to off-load timber directly from rail waggons.

British Isles with an output of 400,000 dozen pairs a year before failing to adapt to the fashion for plastic heels and closing in 1967.[21]

Three companies which have expanded into new products deserve a more extended notice— Henry Venables, Spic and Span Polishes, and W.H. Dorman.

Henry Venables, son of a Stafford bricklayer, was a jobbing carpenter in the 1850s. His premises in Foregate adjoined Bostock's shoe manufactory, and he turned to making their wooden boxes in which shoes were packed for export. It was a small family business. His children recalled that, after they came home from school, it was their job to line the boxes. When Bostocks began making their own boxes about 1863, Henry Venables took up the timber trade, buying and felling trees, from new premises on Doxey Road leased from Lord Stafford. Railway sidings came right into the yard and round timber could be lifted directly into the sawmill. In recent years the company has established a reputation for supplying timber for special projects like repairing

the roof of York Minster after lightning damage, building a replica Globe Theatre in London, and constructing a Shakespearean village on the outskirts of Tokyo. In the 1990s the company has become associated with Chantler Timber.[22]

Spic and Span Polishes Ltd. was established in Glover Street in 1932 to make shoe polishes. In 1938 Dr. H. Simon joined the company, which then diversified into chemical waterproofing products, additives which allowed concrete to be laid in frost, special paints and, later, adhesives and sealants. In 1940 the company was renamed Evode Chemical Works Ltd. and in 1954 opened a new factory in Common Road on the site of the old Stafford Brickworks. In post-war years a series of amalgamations led to the formation of the Evode Group Ltd. and the expansion of its Common Road factory. In 1993 the company was taken over by Laporte,[23] and in December 1996, by the French company Elf Atochem.

W.H. Dorman, the son of a Stafford Congregational minister, began making knives for the shoe industry in 1870. By 1897 the company was producing a range of cutting machines and transferred this business to the British United Shoe Manufacturers Co. The main company produced printing machinery, early refrigerators, and, after 1903, car engines. The company took over the Redbridge Motor Works and with it the Adams aero-engine. During the First World War they developed the Interrupter Gear which allowed machine guns to fire between the blades of a revolving propeller.

In 1927 the company built its first diesel engine and in 1929 started to move to a new factory on the Tixall Road laid out for mass production of engines. They acquired the firm of W.G. Bagnall, locomotive builders, in 1959 and two years later joined the English Electric Company. Today the company trades as Perkins Engines Ltd.[24]

From the late 19th century heavy engineering, initially attracted by good railway freight connections, has become increasingly important as a source of employment in the town. By 1920 there were more workers in engineering than in the shoe trade.

In 1875 W.G. Bagnall came from Wolverhampton to take over a small millwright's business in Castle Street. In the following year he built his first locomotive. The company went on to build steam, diesel and electric locomotives for railways all over the world. In 1959 the company was bought by Dormans, who ended locomotive production two years later.[25]

In 1893 W.O. Rooper transferred part of his emery wheel and grindstone business to Stafford. After several amalgamations, the company became The Universal Grinding Wheel Co. Ltd. and opened a factory equipped with

50 A lorry belonging to W.H. Dorman decorated for the Infirmary procession, *c.*1920, carrying engines made by the company. The photograph was taken in the yard of the original Foregate Street factory.

51 Inside W.H. Dorman's Tixall Road factory in the 1930s. The notice high up near the roof reads, 'Remember it costs £2 a minute to run this factory. Please do not waste a minute.'

52 An advertising card showing a colliery locomotive built at W.G. Bagnall's Castle Engine Works.

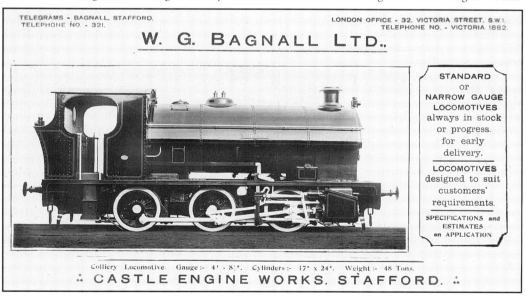

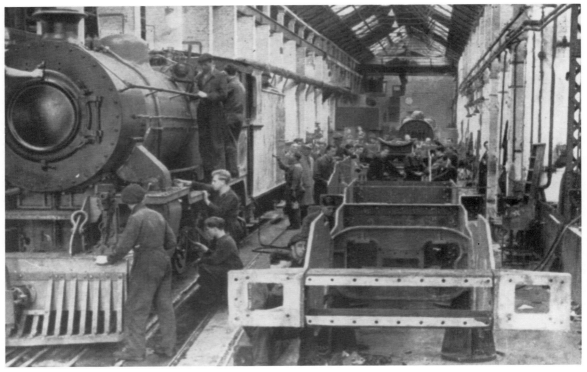

53   The erecting shop at W.G. Bagnall Ltd. in 1950.

the latest machinery at Doxey in 1913. Since then the company has expanded. By the 1970s it was Europe's largest manufacturer of abrasives and grinding wheels, used for everything from tracing delicate patterns on crystal glass to machining special metals for aircraft production. There is also an extensive research laboratory.[26]

The Siemen brothers began manufacturing electrical equipment in Germany in 1847. By 1863 they had a factory in Woolwich and by 1900 they were looking for a site with good rail links and room for expansion. Stafford was attractive and, when the Hough estate adjoining the railway came on the market, they bought it. The Dynamo works, to replace the Woolwich factory, opened in 1903. The wages offered, 39s. for a 52-hour week for a skilled man, were high and this encouraged 800 Woolwich workers and their families to move to Stafford, where they caused a housing and school crisis. To help their workers, the company laid out the Siemen's estate

and built 88 houses there, including larger houses in Salt Avenue intended for foremen.

The factory built not only generators and electric motors but also a wide range of electrical goods from locomotives to domestic appliances. When war broke out in 1914 the company was suspect because of its German connections—one manager, on holiday when the war started, was called up as a German reservist. The company was taken over by the Custodian of Enemy Property and turned over to war work, including the manufacture of shells.

The factory had never been profitable and in 1919 it was sold to the English Electric Company, a merger of several electrical engineering companies. Business problems continued and both production and the number of employees declined. In 1930 George Nelson (later Lord Nelson of Stafford) joined the company and transformed it into a successful enterprise. From his residence at New Hough

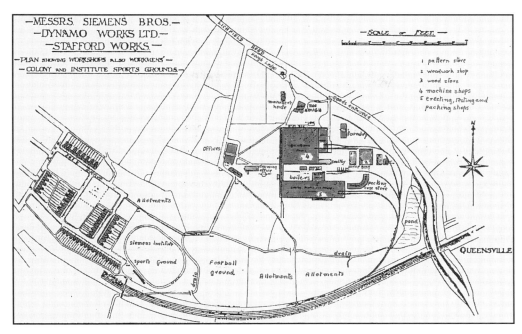

54 Plan of Siemen Bros.' Works and estate in 1905.

55 Siemen Bros.' factory about 1907 showing pre-formed coils being wound into stators of low voltage electric motors. The foremen can be picked out by their jackets and ties.

56 Inside the foundry at The English Electric Company works showing non-ferrous castings being produced by the old green-sand process about 1925.

57 Covenanter tanks being built at The English Electric Company in 1940. On the right are turrets waiting to be fitted.

58 Decorations in The English Electric Company's factory to celebrate Victory after the Second World War. Note the tin hats hanging on the wall.

with a garden gate leading directly into the factory, he gave personal attention to every detail of the work. During the war years the factory built tanks for the army, bombs for the RAF and a range of electrical equipment and castings for the war effort.

After the war the business expanded steadily. A new transformer factory was opened in 1960 and a further factory to make meters and precision measuring devices in St Leonard's Avenue in 1962. Dorman's and its subsidiary W.G. Bagnall Ltd. were taken over in 1961. In 1968 the company merged with The General Electric Company and became simply GEC. This resulted in a re-organisation of work and some job losses. By the late 1970s the number of employees had declined from a peak of 11,000 to little more than 8,000. Since then the company has again faced difficult times and a further amalgamation has taken place. It is now GEC Alsthom.[27]

59 *Right.* Winding a 25-cycle stator for a 30,000 kw 25/50 cycle frequency changer for Victoria, Australia, at The English Electric Co. works, *c.*1950.

60 *Below.* An aerial view of the British Reinforced Concrete Engineering Company factory about 1930.

61 Making salt at Mangers Salt Works Ltd. On the left a salt-maker is filling tubs and on the far right is a common salt open pan.

The last of the engineering companies to be attracted by Stafford's rail links was the British Reinforced Concrete Engineering Company, designers of reinforced concrete structures and makers of welded steel mesh for reinforcing concrete. The company moved from Manchester to Stafford in 1926 when they built a factory at Silkmore Farm adjoining the railway. In 1977 over 750 people were employed but in the 1980s the business declined and the works closed in 1991.[28]

The only other notable industry in the town, until recently, was salt making. Brine had been discovered beneath Stafford Common in 1877 during the search for a water supply for the town. In 1893 the Stafford Salt and Alkali Company was formed to exploit these deposits with a salt-making works near Stafford Common station. In the early 20th century other works were opened and a pipe line was built to carry brine across the town. These activities led to subsidence at the north end of Stafford and in 1970 a court order banned further brine pumping and salt making.[29]

In recent years the proportion of people employed in Stafford's traditional industries has declined very sharply. To attract new businesses, industrial estates have been opened on the outskirts of the town and a variety of new companies like Schott Glass, which came to Drummond Road in 1976 to make laboratory ware and other kinds of special glass, have established themselves. In the 1990s the Corporation has been giving much thought to developing land close to the railway, taking advantage of Stafford's rail link with Europe.

However, the greatest growth has been in clerical and professional work with the County and Borough Councils and in various service and distributive companies.

CHAPTER FIVE

Public Services

In the 18th century the Corporation levied no rates and its income came almost entirely from rents of town property, fines imposed by its courts and tolls from the market. Out of this they endeavoured to maintain St Mary's Church and the grammar school, supervise the market, preside over courts, support the poor and enforce by-laws for health and safety. The service they provided was severely limited and often inadequate. Much of it had to be supplemented by voluntary or charitable aid.

For example, because of the risk of fire there were by-laws to stop people 'taking tobacco' in streets, barns and stables, but the only fire-fighting equipment in 1700 was 27 leather buckets kept in the council house.[1] When fire engines which produced a jet of water by hand pumping from a bucket-filled tank were first made in the 1720s the town quickly acquired one— probably by public subscription with a contribution from the Sun Insurance Company. A more powerful engine was bought, again by public subscription, in 1743.[2] There were no paid firemen. Volunteers to fill the tank and pump the engine had to be called for at every fire.

From an early date the town had been divided into three wards, each based on one of the town gates, and the inhabitants were supposed to provide a watch for their gate. By the 18th century this had lapsed. There were no paid watchmen or police, although the borough court appointed three unpaid constables each year. Voluntary associations, like The Stafford Association for the Prosecution of Felons, offered rewards for information that enabled its members to recover stolen property and prosecute thieves.[3] If serious disturbances took place, as they did in

1800 when the price of bread was high and a mob looted bakers' shops in the town and threatened their owners unless they reduced the price of loaves, troops had to be called out to restore order.[4]

At the beginning of the 18th century, poor relief was still controlled by the Corporation, with one of the town chamberlains acting as overseer. Public relief was supplemented by charitable bequests in many late 17th-century wills. For example, Izaak Walton bequeathed to the town a rent charge on his property. Each

62 A bust of Izaak Walton in St Mary's Church. Every year flowers are placed on it and a special service held to commemorate his birthday on 9 August.

year £10 was used to apprentice two poor boys, £5 to provide a dowry for a poor honest man's daughter, and any surplus to buy coals for the poor. Sir Martin Noell, a London merchant born in Stafford, built and gave to the town the almshouses that still stand in Mill Street. The houses were reserved for the aged poor and the Corporation used various other bequests to provide those living there with a small pension and an allowance of coal. In 1702 the Corporation itself bought four small cottages in Eastgate Street to let rent free to the aged poor from the town.[5]

63 The main entrance to Sir Martin Noell's almshouses built in the 17th century.

The cost of poor relief rose steadily until it could no longer be financed by the Corporation. In 1728 responsibility was handed over to the combined vestries of St Mary and St Chad, who levied annual poor rates on all the inhabitants. Resentment against the rate led the vestry to keep costs as low as possible. Warm clothing given to the poor was to be a special colour or have a coloured patch so that the wearer would be instantly recognised as on poor relief. In 1738 a house on the south side of the churchyard was made into a workhouse for the poor. Everyone in it, including any child over the age of five, had to spin, knit, or do useful work about the house.[6] Later, instead of paying the master or mistress of the workhouse a salary, he or she was paid a weekly amount for each inmate and allowed to keep the profit from any work done. A visitor in 1806 was appalled,

> The poor, 17 in number, are farmed at 3s. 3d. per head per week, washing, soap and firing included. The building is very old, almost tumbling down, the rooms small, the ceilings low, the bedding old and dirty ... about four years ago a fever broke out in it and out of 48 persons 22 died.[7]

The Corporation's financial difficulties worsened at the beginning of the 19th century. The 16th-century Shire Hall, used by the Corporation as well as the County Magistrates, had become dilapidated. In 1794 the magistrates decided to rebuild it and the Corporation had to find £1,000 as their share of the cost.

New members of the Corporation had always been elected by existing members. In the 1820s, claims that these elections had all been carried out in an illegal manner were upheld by the courts. The decision made the election of every member of the Corporation invalid and effectively dissolved it. A fresh charter naming new aldermen and capital burgesses had to be obtained in 1827. Legal costs had been high. Property was mortgaged and economies made but in the early 1830s half the Corporation's income was being used to pay the interest on its debts.[8]

64 *Right.* The Shire Hall built in 1795-8 to a design by John Harvey. It was set back behind the previous hall to allow the Market Square to be opened out.

65 *Left.* The Staffordshire Infirmary in 1837, showing the portico added in 1829 at the expense of Thomas Mottershaw of Silkmore Hall and re-erected in front of the Congregational Church in the 1890s.

At the same time the town was expanding and its population growing fast. Improvements had to come from outside the Corporation. In 1830 an Improvement Commission was set up by an Act of Parliament. All those with property worth more than £25 a year were to be commissioners with power to levy a rate to pave, watch, light, clean and maintain streets—the Corporation retaining some responsibility for the main street and Market Square. The Commission took over the town fire engines and appointed Robert Crewe to maintain them and train 20 volunteers. Wintertime gas lighting was provided in the town centre. Plans for a paid police force and night watch were rejected by those who refused to approve a rate sufficient to meet the cost. Little was done to improve the cleanliness of the streets.

Other services also came about without the involvement of the Corporation. In 1765 the gentlemen of the county subscribed to an infirmary. A house in Foregate was leased and an adjoining house presented to the infirmary by John Eld of Seighford Hall. A matron, apothecary and surgeon were appointed and local doctors gave their services without charge. An infirmary cow and 'a carriage hung upon springs for the conveyance of the sick and maimed' were bought. Every subscriber was entitled to nominate a patient to be treated free. Such was the demand for treatment that the houses were outgrown by 1769. Three years later a purpose-built hospital was opened in Foregate, the £3,000 cost having been raised by public subscription.[9]

66   The men's surgical ward (later Anson Ward) at the Infirmary in 1926.

In 1687 the Corporation leased the site of the old house of correction in the North Gate to the county. The County Gaol was here for the next 100 years but became increasingly over-crowded as the population of the county rose. In 1789 John Howard, the prison reformer, reported, 'In the dungeon for male prisoners I saw 52 chained down, hardly 14 inches being allowed to each'. A new gaol, incorporating all the latest ideas on prison regimes, was opened by the County Magistrates in 1793. After the use of transporta-tion for prisoners ceased, the number of prisoners rose. An extension increased its capacity to 220 men and women but by 1820 the numbers had reached 300. In the 1830s further extensions were made and tread wheels added to make prisoners labour to pump water up to tanks on the roof. By 1850 there were 650 prisoners.[10]

The number of those claiming poor relief was also rising steadily. All over England rate-payers complained about the cost. Stafford was no different from other towns. In 1834 the government decided on reform and passed The Poor Law Amendment Act. This took poor relief out of the hands of existing local bodies and set up a new locally elected Board of Guardians to administer relief which was to be paid for by a local rate. But, and this was a radical change, they would have to act in accordance with detailed regulations laid down centrally and enforced by regular inspection.

New workhouses were built for each group of parishes. In them conditions were deliberately austere to deter people from going there. Relief outside the workhouses was drastically curtailed. At Stafford, the new workhouse north of the town was opened in 1838 and the cost of poor relief cut from £4,963 a year in 1836 to £3,122 in 1838.[11]

In the 1830s the government also turned to the reform of town corporations. The Municipal Corporations Act of 1835 created a new Corpo-ration in Stafford consisting of a mayor, six aldermen and 18 councillors. Councillors, unlike the old capital burgesses, were to be elected by all ratepaying householders every three years.

67 A plan of the County Gaol in 1856 showing
the Crescent building added in 1832 and the
'new male prison' built in the 1850s.

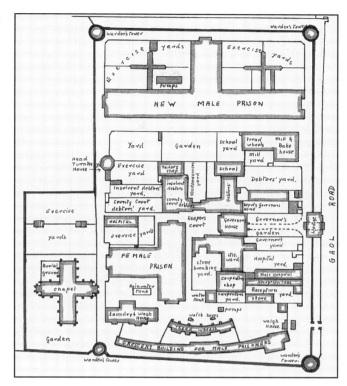

68 Stafford Gaol in 1905 with some of the
staff lined up outside. At one time public
executions took place on the roof of the main
gate on the right. The towers in the distance
housed warders' quarters.

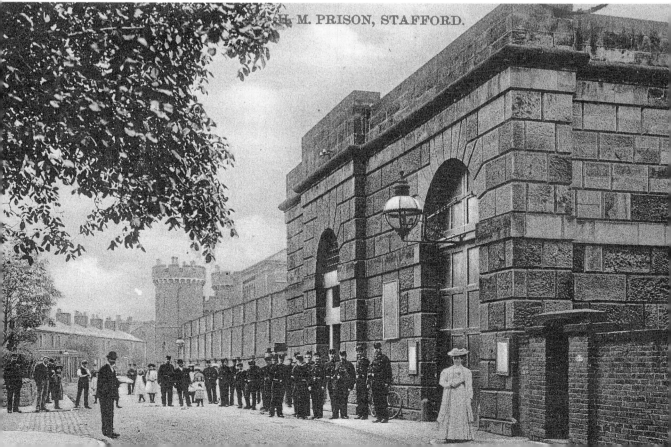

H. M. PRISON, STAFFORD.

69 *Above*. The Union Workhouse built in 1837–8 in Marston Road. In 1948 it became Fernleigh old people's home and a hospital for the chronically sick.

70 *Left*. The Guild Hall in Market Square is on the right in this 1859 print.

All new corporations were required to appoint a police force. Stafford ignored this requirement until 1840, when they reluctantly appointed a chief constable, a sergeant, and two constables. In order to reduce the cost, they suggested to the Improvement Commissioners that the chief constable should also be in charge of fire engines, and that the Commissioners should pay part of his salary in respect of these duties.[12]

The new Corporation inherited the debts of the old. Some property was sold and money raised by mortgages, but the Corporation's financial problems continued. About 1850 the mace and other Corporation insignia were seized as security for unpaid debts. A full-scale inquiry followed, and its report in 1852 marks a turning point in the finances of local government in the town.[13]

After 1852 a borough rate was charged on all property owners at a level which allowed for the provision of public services as well as the reduction of debt. In the same year, the Corporation gave up their share of the Shire Hall and, in return, the County Magistrates paid for a Guild Hall incorporating a police station on the western side of Market Square, where *The Star Inn* had stood. A tunnel-like entrance led to a yard with police barracks on one side and a new covered market on the far side. This replaced the market behind the Shire Hall.[14] In 1867 the market was extended by covering in the yard and demolishing the police barracks to make an entrance in Crabbery Street. The name St John's Market was given to the extended market.[15]

In the 1830s Stafford was both dirty and unhealthy. In the main street, drainage was still by a channel in the centre of the road. In the poorer districts, drainage was non-existent. Houses had cess pits. Refuse was not collected. In poorer areas, vegetable refuse was thrown into the street and left to putrefy.[16] Larger houses with stables and pigsties piled manure at the side of their back street. Regular cattle markets were held in Gaolgate (often called Cow Street at the time) and both pigs and sheep were sold in Eastgate. The town's water supply came from private and public wells, but the soil was so saturated by leakage from cess pits that almost all the water was contaminated. Fevers were endemic. A visiting judge declared Stafford to be 'the most stinking town I was ever in in my life'.[17]

The Improvement Commission had power to remove nuisances but rarely used it. A branch of the Health of Towns Association, formed in the town in 1847, failed to overcome opposition from those who objected to paying additional rates. Before 1853, the Corporation had no money to do more than macadamise the main street and fit hand pumps on the tops of public wells so that rubbish could not be tipped into them.[18]

After 1853, the Corporation was increasingly concerned with health but, until they became a Board of Health in 1872, had limited powers. The first Medical Officer of Health was

71 Cattle waiting to be sold in Gaolgate during a May Fair in the 1890s.

appointed in 1874 and a start made on replacing cesspits with privies on a tub system. The Corporation provided an emptying service. This was supposed to be done at night but the tubs on open carts were on the streets 'sufficiently late to sicken professional men going to business, and sufficiently early in the evening to destroy the pleasure that wearied workers have sought from a walk in the cool of the coming night'.[19] A sanitary department was opened at Lammascote in 1879 and a start made on laying main sewers in the following year. By 1897, when the town's first sewage works was opened, all the streets had sewers and about a third of all houses were connected to them.[20]

Private smithfields at *The Sun* in Lichfield Road, *The Talbot* in Victoria Road and the *Junction Inn* in Newport Road slowly replaced cattle markets in the street, although the annual

May cattle fair lingered on in Gaolgate Street until 1909, in spite of protests about 'disgusting filth' and causing 'alarm and terror to the ladies of the town'.

In the 1870s the Corporation began to extend its powers and provide a much wider range of public services. It had taken the powers of a Local Board of Health in 1872. Three years later the Improvement Commission was dissolved and its powers transferred to the Corporation. Most important of all, in 1876 The Stafford Corporation Act enabled new services to be provided and existing private projects taken over. The Borough Hall was built in Eastgate Street in 1877, providing much needed office accommodation. In 1906 the posts of town clerk and borough treasurer were made full time because of the increase in work to be done.

In 1876 the Corporation acquired the cemetery on the Eccleshall Road, opened by the Burial Board in 1856. In the same year a volunteer fire brigade was formed to take over the old Improvement Commission engines. A new fire station at the corner of Greengate Street and South Walls followed in 1885. Two years later, a steam-powered pump replaced the hand pumps which had proved unable to reach the roofs of three-storeyed buildings during a serious fire in Gaolgate. The first motorised engine, which did not have to wait for horses to be caught and harnessed before it turned out, was bought in 1913.[21]

In 1879 the Corporation bought a private bathhouse at the end of Friars Walk from Lord Stafford and, in 1892, replaced it with public brine baths near Green Bridge, next to the fire station and incorporating an open-sided tower for drying fire hoses. The title Royal Brine Baths was granted after a visit by the Duchess of Teck in 1895.[22]

72 The Borough Hall in Eastgate Street. When the Council offices moved to Riverside it was adapted and refurbished as *The Gatehouse*.

Municipal Buildings and Borough Hall, Stafford.

73 *Above.* The Mayor's Parlour in the Borough Hall in 1932.

74 *Below left.* The fire station and one of the engines in 1927. Ernest Haywood, the Captain of the Brigade, was made a Freeman of the Borough when he eventually retired in 1942.

75 *Below right.* The corner of Gaolgate and Market Square after the fire in October 1887. The failure of the town's manual engines to deal with the fire effectively led to the purchase of the town's first steam fire engine.

76 The Royal Brine Baths in 1920. In front of the building was a cycle shop occupied by Martin Mitchell and a tobacco kiosk occupied by his daughter who published this postcard view.

The Corporation planned a town water works in 1877 and began the search for a supply of pure water. Several bore holes unexpectedly sank into salt deposits and had to be abandoned. Eventually a supply was found at Milford and the works there opened in 1890.

The privately owned gasworks, begun in 1829 by William Edwards & Co. in Gas Lane, were bought in 1878. The Corporation also opened its own electricity works in Foregate Street in 1895. At first this provided lighting to 36 houses and shops. At weekends the generators shut down and premises were supplied by batteries.

The Free Libraries and Museums Act was adopted in 1879. A museum was opened in an extension to the Borough Hall and a lending library in the former dining room there. In 1914 the Carnegie Trust made a grant towards a new library and museum building at the corner of Newport Road. An art gallery was added in 1934.

In the 19th century there were many complaints that the town mill's dam caused flooding upstream. The Corporation therefore bought the mill from Lord Stafford in 1879, with the intention of demolishing it. They were then advised that a new weir and floodgates would control flooding more effectively. The mill survived until 1957.[23]

One area liable to flood was the low lying land opposite the railway station. This land was bought by the Corporation and its level raised by tipping. It was laid out as Victoria Park in 1908. An extension with a bowling green was

77 The Borough Free Library built in 1914 with aid from a donation from Andrew Carnegie.

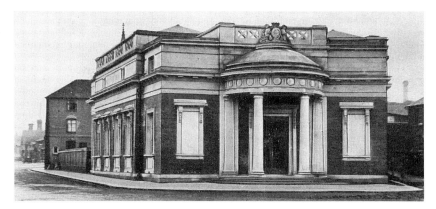

78 *Left.* The Town Mill about 1905. There was a water-powered mill working on this site from early times until 1957. The mill has now been pulled down but the water wheels are preserved in an extension to Victoria Park.

79 *Below.* The opening of the extension to Victoria Park, on the town side of the river, in 1911 to commemorate the Coronation of King George V.

Police Barracks, Stafford.

80   The Police Barracks in Park Street in 1923. The site is now the headquarters of the County Library.

added to mark the Coronation of George V and a further extension with a paddling pool for children opened in 1930.

The County Magistrates and their county police force absorbed the borough police in 1858 but, except for the Shire Hall and County Gaol, had little other visible presence in Stafford. The Local Government Act of 1888 replaced them with an elected County Council, which bought up all the property on one side of Martin Street as a site for their new offices and council chamber. These opened in 1895. Eastgate House, on the corner of Martin Street, was the only building retained. It became the home of the Chief Constable. The County Gaol was closed in 1916 but reopened to house Irish prisoners taken during the Easter Rising.[24] Later the warders' quarters were used briefly as council flats in the post-1918 housing shortage. The Home Office reopened the prison in 1939.[25]

Since 1945, the borough has often been seen as too small a unit to provide adequate services. The old borough fire brigade, for example, became part of the National Fire Service in 1941 to meet wartime emergencies. In 1948 it was handed back, but to the County Council as part of a new County Fire Service. In 1971 a new fire station was opened off Queensway, replacing the wartime station in Water Street. In the 1970s the Borough Library, Museum and Art Gallery were absorbed by the county. The library is part of the County Library Service, the museum has disappeared, and the art gallery transferred and expanded in the old Shire Hall. In 1948 the National Assistance Act ended a separate poor relief and gave the County Council a new Social Services Department to take over some poor relief functions and provide a much expanded and more humane service. The old workhouse was refurbished as Fernleigh Old

81 Martin Street, *c*.1890. All the property on the left of the picture was demolished when the County Buildings were erected in 1895.

82 The Council Chamber, County Buildings, in 1932.

83 This photograph, smuggled out of Stafford Gaol, shows Irish Republican Brotherhood prisoners, captured at Dublin and Enniscorthy after the Easter Rising in 1916, in one of the prison yards.

84 *Above.* St John's Market in 1950.

85 *Below.* Statistics of the work of the Borough Council in 1995/6.

DID YOU KNOW —

Stafford Borough Council covers an area of 230 sq. miles with a population of over 122,000. The Borough stretches from Trentham in the north, almost to Uttoxeter in the east, to Newport in the west, and almost to Cannock in the south.

Stafford Borough Council provides:

7164 Houses and Flats

1099 Sheltered Dwellings

673 Warden Linked Homes

323 Lifeline Linked Dwellings

Stafford Borough Council:

Recycles 700 tonnes of glass each year

Empties 50,000 wheeled bins every week

Sweeps 9,000 km of roads every year

In a year, at Stafford Borough Council's Recreation Centres:

375,000 Tickets are sold for swimming

70,000 People attend Keep Fit and Weight Training Sessions

18,000 Games of Squash are played

14,000 Games of Badminton are played

People's Home and Hospital, later replaced by Foxwalls Home and Kingsmead Hospital. As a result of these and other changes the need of the County Council for offices has grown rapidly. The other side of Martin Street, Tipping Street and part of Eastgate have been acquired and built over.

Other services have been reorganised on a regional basis. The Midland Electricity Board took over the Corporation Electricity Company in 1948 and the West Midland Gas Board the Corporation gas works in 1949. In 1974 the Severn Trent Water Authority took over the Corporation water and sewage works. All these services have been extensively reorganised since being taken over by larger authorities.

The Corporation itself has extensively modernised its services and in 1974 the area it administered was enlarged to include Stone and a sprawling rural area. New Civic Offices were opened in 1978 and the old Borough Hall refurbished as The Gatehouse Theatre Complex. Mr. Murt's field has become Rowley Park Sports Stadium with a running track, bowling green, tennis courts and sports pitches. The old Royal Brine Baths were demolished in 1974 and replaced by The Riverside Recreation and Leisure Centre. The Guild Hall and St John's Market have been redeveloped, after prolonged opposition from market stall holders. The changes are too numerous to chronicle in detail.

Today the public services are more extensive than at any time in the history of the town but their ever increasing cost is beginning to cause concern.

CHAPTER SIX

The Changing Town

During the 18th century the population of Stafford more than doubled. By the time of the first Census in 1801 there were 3,898 people and 723 houses in the town. Much of the increase had taken place in the latter part of the century, when workmen were attracted by the growth in the manufacture of shoes. Even before this the county town was prosperous enough for John Stevenson, a Stafford mercer, to open a bank in 1737. This was one of the earliest banks outside London and came to be known as The Old Bank. In 1866 it became part of Lloyd's Bank[1] and

their Market Square premises still carry the name Old Bank on its frontage.

The rising population was almost all contained within the line of the medieval town walls. Comparison of the 1788 town map with the early 17th-century map by John Speed shows how the area within the walls had been filled in. In particular, Broadeye, once occupied only by scattered dwellings, was becoming a populous area. John Wright built a wind-powered corn mill here in 1796 using some of the stone auctioned off when the old Shire Hall was

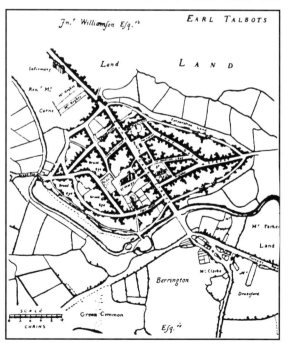

86 *Above left.* The Old Bank, formerly Stevenson, Salt & Co. now Lloyds, in the 1930s.

87 *Above right.* A map of Stafford in 1788 drawn up for the Stafford estate.

88 The windmill at Broadeye had lost its sails by the time this photograph was taken soon after 1900. The houses on the left have been pulled down and the site added to Victoria Park.

demolished. An iron plate inscribed 'I.W. 1796' can still be seen on the tower of the mill.[2]

Visitors comments that the town was a 'dull, idle place' with inns 'fit only for market people'[3] seem rather harsh. Around the turn of the century Stafford presented a lively social scene, at least for the well-to-do. The diversion of the main post road through the town in 1785 brought more travellers and greater prosperity to inn-keepers. At the same time William Horton, the shoe manufacturer, had struck up a friendship with Richard Brindsley Sheridan, M.P. for the town, playwright and part owner of the Theatre Royal in London. Sheridan was a prominent figure in London society. Horton's gifts eased Sheridan's unending financial difficulties and in

return he brought the 'wits and bright spirits of the age' to Stafford. There were parties at Chetwynd House, Horton's home, where Horton's brother sang specially composed songs. London fashions were seen on the streets of Stafford. Six ladies were known as 'the illustrious groupe' and there was talk of a 'galaxy of other beauties'.[4]

Horse races on Coton Fields had taken place each October since 1763. Now race week became a social occasion. Sheridan stayed with Horton and acted as one of the race stewards. Twice in the 1790s the Prince Regent came down for the races.[5]

Horton was one of a group who built a small theatre in Martin Street which was leased to Samuel Stanton and his company. Visiting London actors appeared there on occasions. It was here, during Race Week in 1794, that Sheridan met Harriot Melon, the 17-year-old daughter of an itinerant actress. Harriot was invited to appear at the Theatre Royal, married a wealthy banker and, after his early death, took as her second husband the Duke of St Albans.[6]

After a time the town reverted to being a market town with no special social pretensions. It grew steadily. By 1821 there were 991 houses and 10 years later 1,286. By 1831 the population had risen to 6,956. Some of this expansion was within the walls, especially in the Eastgate/Back Walls area, but most of it in a growing suburb north of the town. When the new County Gaol opened in 1793 the North Gate, no longer required as a prison, was taken down. This created an open space which came to be called Gaol Square, with Gaol Road providing a way to the new gaol and beyond. Houses were built in Brownings Lane; County Road and New Street were laid out by 1835; Friar Street, Cross Street and Fancy Walk a few years later. The occupants were almost all employed in the manufacture of shoes and the early factories were in this area. As the population grew, a school was opened in 1825 and a church in 1839.

In 1834, White's *Directory* described the well-paved main street as 'containing many well stocked shops and several excellent inns' as well as 'noble specimens of antique half-timbered houses'.[7] George Borrow, who was employed as an ostler at the *Swan Inn* for a short time, described it as

> a place of infinite life and bustle. Travellers were continually stopping at it; and, to attend to their wants and minister to their convenience, an army of servants was kept; waiters, chambermaids, grooms, postilions, shoe-blacks, cooks, scullions and what-not, for there was a barber and hairdresser who had been at Paris and talked French with a cockney accent.[8]

Market Square was still a market.

> On market day all the space was occupied with market stalls, mostly canvas covered, except where the farmers' wives and daughters sat in rows behind their baskets endeavouring to tempt the ladies of Stafford to purchase eggs, poultry and other farm produce.[9]

Cattle were sold in Gaolgate, and at the winter fair women and girls, hoping to be hired as servants for the coming year, stood along the pavements waiting to be offered a place. At the corner of Eastgate Street and Market Street was

89 A print showing Market Square in 1859. The gun was presented to the town after it was captured from the Russians during the Crimean War. It was later moved to Pitcher Bank and finally to Grosvenor Park in Chester.

the pig market with pens on the south side, and at the corner of Eastgate Street and Diglake (Tipping Street) was the open-air crockery market.

To the south, the 1835 Municipal Corporations Act had extended the town boundary to include Forebridge, where additional houses were beginning to be built. A small number of houses was also constructed along Lichfield Road as far as Spittal Brook, renamed Queensville in 1838 to mark Queen Victoria's coronation.

The Grand Junction Railway, opened in 1837, skirted the town, with a station on the far side of the river reached by an access road from the Newport Road. Later, when Stafford became the border station between the North and South divisions of the LNWR, locomotives as well as

their drivers, firemen and guards changed there on through trains. By 1860 both the station and its approach road had become inadequate.

A new station was built in 1862, and in 1866 a second bridge across the Sow, with a new road from Earl Street to the station, was constructed to provide a better access from the town centre. The growing number of railway employees living in the town led to the building of a whole new suburb close to the station but outside the borough boundary. At first this was called New Town but was better known as Castletown. A school was opened there in 1863 and a church, dedicated to St Thomas, in 1866.[10]

The town continued to grow. By 1871 the population was over 14,000, and by 1881 almost 20,000. Most of the new houses were at the

90   A postcard view of Market Square during the May Fair in 1902. Cattle are being sold in Gaolgate while a pleasure fair occupies Market Square.

91 Victoria Road looking towards the station in 1907. The photographic studio and shop on the left belonged to Weiss & Fowkes.

north end of the town, where new streets were laid out and vacant plots in existing streets built upon to provide homes for those who worked in the shoe factories. The *Staffordshire Advertiser* reported in 1873 that in the Rowley Street area 'a new population has sprung up within the last 12 or 14 years so that a large area which, within the memory of those who are still young, was pasture land and gardens is now covered with houses and shoe factories'.[11] Albert, Victoria and Peel Terraces all date from about 1860: Lovatt, Rowley, Lloyd, Wogan and Marsh Streets are a little later.

By this time the townspeople were becoming aware of the need for better housing in the interest of public health. In 1874 the Corporation adopted the Local Government Act and with it by-laws laying down minimum standards for setting out streets, providing drainage, and building houses with space for air to circulate. The first street laid out under the new regulations was Tillington Street, reported in 1875 to be '36 feet wide and sewered with a good fall'.[12]

The standard of living of many working men and their families was rising. The more prosperous could think of raising money to buy or build their own home. The first building society in the town was The Stafford Permanent Benefit Society formed in 1867. The Stafford Railway Building Society was incorporated 10 years later. Other societies bought land, laid out roads and building plots and helped members build on them. In this way the Conservative Land Society laid out Talbot, Ingestre and Shrewsbury Roads in the late 1860s.[13]

About the same time other streets were formed and houses built in the Friars Terrace—Wolverhampton Road area up to the railway line. Beyond the railway, the Stafford Land Building and Improvement Company bought the Rowley Hall estate in 1866 and laid out a model suburb

92 *Left*. Rowley Hall, built by William Keen about 1812, photographed in 1868 when it was occupied by Robert Hand, solicitor. It is now a private hospital.

93 *Right*. The first council houses built in Broadeye, photographed by A.P. Baggs in the 1970s for the *Victoria County History of Staffordshire*, vol. vi.

of plots for 'residences of a superior class' on part of the land. The suburb was to have its own church and private pleasure gardens. The building plots failed to sell and in 1871 the shareholders divided the remaining land between themselves and wound up the company. The pleasure gardens still exist but the church was never built, although St John's Road is named after it.[14]

The Stafford Corporation Act (1876), besides enlarging the powers of the Corporation, also extended the boundary of the borough to bring in built up areas like Castletown as well as areas such as Coton Field, Littleworth and part of the Newport Road, where future building might be expected.

Between 1876 and 1914 Stafford expanded along each of the main roads out of town. The population rose to 25,000 and the number of houses to over 4,500. Most new houses were solidly built and builders proudly put up date stones which help to date the roads today—1882 in Cramer Street, 1884 in Rowley Grove, 1895 in The Oval, 1908 in Cambridge Street, 1910 in St George's Road, are a few of those still to be seen.

Legal wrangles over the future of Coton Field were settled in 1880. This released some land for building, while preserving most of it for allotments for burgesses.[15] As a result, Corporation Street was laid out in the 1890s, opening the way for later developments to the east of Stafford.

In 1901 the Corporation built the first nine council houses in Broadeye. These had a scullery, living room and two bedrooms for a rent of

4s. 3d. per week. Other council houses in Crooked Bridge Road, Coton Field and Lammascote followed. By 1914, 100 houses were occupied and another 40 were being built.[16]

In 1903 Siemen Bros. transferred their Woolwich factory to Stafford and brought with them 800 workers and their families. This influx caused a housing shortage in the town. Siemens themselves planned an estate for some of the workers and built 88 three-bedroomed houses and two-bedroomed flats in Siemens Road, Sabine Street and Lawrence Avenue, as well as larger houses for their foremen in Salt Avenue.

The estate was never completed because the profits of the company were insufficient, but more houses were added in 1924.[17]

In the centre of the town, the building of the County Technical School and Education Offices gave the opportunity to set back the building line and create Victoria Square. In 1922 this provided a site for the borough's War Memorial. The figure of a soldier on it originally faced the railway station, from which the men had departed, but, after the building of the new Crown Courts, the soldier did an about-turn and now faces St Mary's Church.

94   The War Memorial in Victoria Square was unveiled in 1922 by Corporal Sturland, a local man who had been seriously wounded at Ypres. This photograph was taken during the Two Minutes' Silence at an Armistice Day service a few years later.

95 *Above*. The Jubilee Fountain, designed by Councillor Wormald, was erected in 1887 to mark Queen Victoria's Golden Jubilee. This view is one of a series of postcards published by W.G. Butters, fine art dealer and picture framer, in 1921.

96 *Left*. The fountain erected in 1889 by the widow of Thomas Sidney to commemorate her husband.

Queen Victoria's Golden Jubilee in 1887 was marked by the erection of an elaborate drinking fountain in Market Square. The project was opposed by those who objected to the loss of space for market stalls. Alderman Followes even attacked it with a hammer and chisel. However, it survived until 1934, when it was removed to allow more space to park cars in the Square. Two years later the widow of Thomas Sidney, a local boy who had been M.P. for the town and also Lord Mayor of London, erected another drinking fountain in Gaol Square in memory of her husband. A clock was added in 1916 and in 1928 the whole was demolished when a van backed into it. A replacement clock on a pillar was put up in 1930 and remained until the building of Queensway in 1976.[18]

The late 19th century saw the beginning of a revolution in shopping. In the 1870s the owner of every main-street shop lived on the premises. Typical was Henry Cliff, who had a grocery shop in Gaolgate. A young man who worked there recalled how chests of tea from India and Ceylon were kept in the attic and every Monday samples were brought down and tea brewed for Mr. Cliff to taste. He then pronounced 'Twopence an ounce' or whatever he thought right, before the assistants weighed it out into bags. Sugar, rice, currants, sago and tapioca also had to be weighed out. Customers brought their own jars to be filled from barrels of syrup and treacle, kept at the top of the yard.[19]

Slowly, retailing changed with branded goods, packed, advertised and priced by the manufacturer. Large companies opened branch shops selling a standard range of products. The first branch shop in Stafford was probably Freeman, Hardy & Willis (shoes) about 1886, followed by Boots the Chemist in 1897, Home and Colonial (grocers and tea dealers) in 1898 and Liptons (also grocery and tea) in 1899.

Another new style of shop was the department store, found in Stafford as early as the 1880s, when such shops were hardly known outside London. In 1743 George Boulton, a draper, had opened a shop on the south side of Market Square. By 1850 this was Boulton, Talbot & Buxton, with a second shop round the corner in Greengate Street and, by the 1880s, Brookfield and Windows. In the 1880s eight shops on the corner of Market Square were pulled down and replaced by their new departmental store, concentrating on ladies' fashions and household furnishings. Other departments were added later.[20]

97 Gaolgate looking towards Gaol Square in 1918, showing typical shops and shop fronts of the period. None of the buildings survive today.

COSTUMIERS, MILLINERS AND GENERAL DRAPERS.
Gentlemens, Youths and Boys Complete Outfitters,
House Furnishers and Removal Contractors.

Where to clothe yourselves, ~ ~ your sons and daughters, or Furnish your ~ home from the kitchen to the attic. ~ ~

Brookfields.....
Patterns, Prices, and Estimates bear favourable comparison and their work is most reliable. - - -

GENTLEMEN'S BRANCH

52, Greengate.

Do not Imagine
that you need go to London for your ~ ~ requirements.

Brookfields.....
have been ~ established at ~ Stafford ~ **OVER 160 YEARS,** they can supply anything; carry out and conduct every description of work.

IRONMONGERY, &c.
CHINA, GLASS, : : :

15 & 16,
GOALGATE.

1, 2, 3, 4, GREENGATE.
6, 7, 8, 9, MARKET SQUARE.

Carpet and Bedding Factory: **EASTGATE.**
Repository: **FOREGATE.**

98 Advertisement for Brookfield's departmental store in 1905.

Also new was the bazaar style of shop, selling a variety of low-priced goods laid out on open counters for customers to select what they wanted. The first of these shops in Stafford was The Empire Bazaar, opened as one of a small chain of shops by George Fitelson in Crabbery Street in 1908. Everything on one counter cost one penny and on the other three pence.

The oldest sports club in the town was Stafford Victoria Cricket Club founded in 1844. This had given way to Stafford Cricket Club by 1864. Stafford Rangers, rugby, hockey and angling clubs all date from the mid-1870s. Golf started in the grounds of Coton Hill Hospital in the 1880s and moved to Stafford Common in 1890. By the end of the century, a roller skating rink had opened in Newport Road and rowing boats could be hired from a boatyard under the Royal Brine Baths.

The theatre in Martin Street was extended in 1877 and refurbished in 1912. In 1915 it was badly damaged by fire and never re-opened. The cinema came to Stafford in 1910 when The Electric Picture Palace opened in Glover Street. 'A commodious building with a sloping floor that will enable every member of the audience to obtain a good view.'[21] The Albert Hall followed in 1912 and the Picture House in Bridge Street in 1914. The Sandonia, which opened as a variety theatre in 1920, became a cinema in 1923. The much larger Odeon, at the junction of Newport and Lichfield Roads, opened in 1936.

In 1914 it was noted that in recent years house building 'had slackened within the borough whilst a large number of houses are erected immediately outside the boundary'.[22] Services had to be provided for these houses and in 1917 the

99 Martin Mitchell, who had a cycle shop at the front of the Royal Brine Baths, hired out rowing boats from this boathouse at the side of the Baths. This postcard dates from 1905.

100 The Picture House in Bridge Street in the early 1920s. The building remained almost unaltered until it closed in 1995.

borough boundary was extended to include them as well as much future building land.

Between the wars, extensive building of mainly semi-detached council houses took place in 'garden city' suburbs at Lammascote, Coton Field, Littleworth, Tithe Barn Road and off the Stone Road. By 1939 there were 1,248 council houses. Private estates were also built north of the town, and by The British Reinforced Concrete Co. at Burton Manor. In 1932 the Corporation was proud that 'areas which a few years ago were green fields are now attractive residential suburbs'.[23] In 1934 the borough boundary was further extended to take in much of Baswich, Highfields, Rickerscote and Moss Pit. By 1941 the town population had risen to 37,750.

Much of this building was sited on the most easily available land. The 1932 Town Planning Act gave the Borough Council some control over where building took place and allowed the relationship between housing and open spaces, shops and industry to be considered. By 1938 Stafford had drawn up its first Operative Planning Scheme.[24]

During the war years, the Borough Council set up a Reconstruction Committee, later renamed The Town Planning Committee, to make plans for the future. In 1947 the County Council was given responsibility for drawing up a long-term development plan under the Town and Country Planning Act and the Borough Council published their ideas to 're-equip and modernise our environment' as a 'basis for discussion and long term planning'.[25]

101   Scale model of proposals for a neighbourhood unit at Baswich in 1945. The proposals were later modified.

A photograph of a Scale Model of the first proposals for the Baswich Neighbourhood Unit. Existing houses are in dark colour and proposed in light.

Reference :—

1. District Centre.	*5. Crematorium.*	*9. River Penk (Radford Bridge).*
2. Eastern Bypass Road.	*6. Cannock Road.*	*10. Public open space.*
3. Cannock Road Bypass.	*7. Lichfield Road.*	*11. Playing Fields.*
4. Future Cemetery.	*8. Canal.*	*12. Sites for Schools.*

102   Council houses being built at Silkmore in 1946-7. Note the deliberate variation in design.

New residential areas were to form a series of neighbourhood units, each with houses for 7,000 or more people, its own shops, community buildings, health centre, primary school and open spaces. Roads would have wide grass verges and shops would be set in 'a pleasant tree shaded walk with seats for rest and flowers and shrubs for visual refreshment'. New industry would be separated from housing and located at Astonfields or close to the railway station.

Ring roads would link existing radial roads to keep through traffic out of the town centre. Within the inner ring road the town centre would be largely rebuilt, keeping only 'a few undoubted architectural treasures'. There would be office zones and shopping areas. Greengate Street would be pedestrianised to keep through traffic off the main street. The main shopping area would be the northern end of the town centre, with many shops in Greengate Street removed to extend Market Square and open up a view of St Mary's Church. A sports centre would be built in the grounds of St George's Hospital, an Arts Centre in Gaol Square, and an Entertainment Precinct,

including a civic restaurant, 'in a sylvan setting on the bank of a revivified river' in Bridge Street. Although many ideas were Utopian, its central principles have been put into effect during the last 50 years.

After the war the Council undertook a crash programme of house building. By 1949 over 1,200 houses had been built. By 1959 there were 5,000 post-war houses in the town, of which the Council had built 3,000. Since then the building of large estates, planned broadly on the lines of neighbourhood units, has continued steadily, so that the town now sprawls far beyond its pre-war boundaries.

In addition, large houses like Highfield Manor (site of High Park) and Silkmore Hall (site of Hall Close) have been pulled down and several smaller houses put up on their sites. Some large houses have survived, but without their grounds. In the late 1940s, the grounds of Burton House were built over by English Electric Co. with houses for employees. In the 1980s, the remaining grounds of Rowley Hall were used for housing, when the hall became a hospital.

103 Part of Burton House Estate designed by E. Bower Norris in the late 1940s for employees of the English Electric Company.

104 Gaol Square in 1951.

In the post-war years, many of the older small houses in the town have been demolished. Slum clearance and rebuilding began in the area north of Browning Street in the 1950s and has continued piecemeal. In Broadeye, the building of Chell Road and other road works destroyed a large number of houses. In Eastgate and Tipping Streets houses have been replaced by public buildings and car parks. The construction of traffic islands at either end of Queensway destroyed other houses. Today there is hardly a single house left in the centre of Stafford.

The town centre has changed more in the last 40 years than at any time since William the Conqueror built a castle here. In the north of the town the medieval road pattern has been erased by Chell Road. Cherry Street has been swallowed by the College of Further Education and Bath Street and Albion Place by the Guildhall development.

In the main shopping streets the number of branches of multiple shops, building societies and banks has continued to grow and, alongside the change, has gone the demolition of old inconvenient shops and their replacement by modern premises with more open floor space. In 1962 the Council agreed with developers for the building of two shopping precincts in the northern part of the town. After bitter opposition from market traders, the redevelopment of the Guild Hall, with the relocation of St John's Market behind a new shopping arcade, has also been completed.

Both Tesco and Sainsbury obtained planning permission for supermarkets on the edge of the shopping area in 1978. Both agreed to build multi-storey car parks as part of the development and to hand them over to the Council. Sainsbury's multi-storey car park was

105 Map of the Broadeye-Gaol Square area in 1900 showing the road pattern which survived until the changes of the last 30 years.

106 Greengate Street, *c*.1910. Some of the buildings still survive although much changed at ground-floor level, others have been demolished.

107 Market Square with flower beds laid out to commemorate the coronation of Elizabeth II.

never built, but money was given to the Council to develop other car parking. A car park was also incorporated in the Guildhall development and in the site for a larger Sainsbury's. These projects have tended to enhance the northern part of the town as a shopping centre—as suggested in the 1948 plan.

Thought has been given to making the town centre a more attractive place. Market Square was laid out with flower beds and trees in 1953 to commemorate the coronation of Queen Elizabeth II. In 1992, as part of the pedestrianisation of the town centre, the Square was paved and given new black and gold street furniture. After so much of central Stafford has been demolished, thought is at last being given to the conservation of buildings such as the High House and old Shire Hall.

CHAPTER SEVEN

Religion

At the beginning of the 16th century England was a Catholic country. The Church was wealthy but had lost the respect of many people. The numerous friaries and monasteries were in decline, with numbers falling and religious devotion at a low ebb.

In Stafford, St Mary's, the principal church with considerable property and income, was served by a dean, a college of prebends and four vicars choral. The dean was usually non-resident and there had been complaints for over a century about the misuse of church funds and neglect of church property, including the deanery and the houses for prebends and vicars choral south of the churchyard. Various small foundations for religious purposes, called chantries, offered regular prayers and masses at the 10 altars within the church, and one supported a school where a few boys of the town received a Latin-based education.

The other town church, St Chad's, had been granted to a prebendary of Lichfield Cathedral, who appointed a curate to serve there. St Chad's had a very small parish and was always poor.

The Franciscans, or Grey Friars, had a house in Foregate and the Austin Friars another near the Green in Forebridge. Two hospitals, St Leonard's and St John's, were endowed to provide care for aged, poor people, but in the 16th-century St John's had not done so within living memory.[1] None of these institutions was wealthy and the town had little benefit from them.

In the 1530s Henry VIII made himself Supreme Head of the Church in England, taking to himself the right to tax the Church, appoint its dignitaries, control its laws and supervise its courts. The Church was cut off from the pope but there was no religious revolution. The changes allowed the king to control the church court that annulled his marriage to Catherine of Aragon and to order the dissolution of friaries and monasteries and confiscation of their property. The inmates of the Stafford friaries were transferred to other church posts, or given small pensions. The buildings and property were sold; those of the Grey Friars to the Dorringtons and those of the Austin Friars to the Stanfords of Rowley Hall.[2]

Other more rapid and far reaching changes followed during the reign of Edward VI, Henry's son. An English Prayer Book and services in English were introduced. Altars were replaced by communion tables. Simple surplices were worn instead of rich vestments. Carved images of saints were destroyed and prayers to them forbidden. Collegiate churches, chantries and hospitals were all dissolved and their property seized.

In Stafford the College ceased to exist. The dean, prebendaries and vicars choral were dismissed, its property seized, and its gold and silver plate confiscated. St Mary's Church was not taken and Thomas Cheddulton, one of the prebendaries, was appointed vicar with one of the vicars choral as his curate. Henry Peckeman, the chantry priest who had kept a school, became the schoolmaster. These three all had small salaries from the Crown. The rest received pensions. Part of the College property was sold to Lord Stafford, part used as an endowment for the school and the rest retained by the Crown.[3] The two hospitals of St Leonard and St John were also dissolved and their buildings and property seized.

England briefly became Catholic under Mary I before the national Protestant church was restored by her sister Elizabeth I. The towns-people seem to have accepted all these changes, although Thomas Cheddulton resigned rather than accept the last of them. In 1570 his successor, Robert Sutton, complained that his salary was not always paid and that expenditure on maintaining the church was inadequate. The Corporation supported his complaint and in 1571 Queen Elizabeth granted them all the College lands remaining in her hands on condition that they paid the rector (previously a vicar), his curate and the schoolmaster and maintained both church and school.[4]

The rector was poorly paid and he usually held a second church post, leaving most of his duties at St Mary's to be carried out by an even more poorly paid curate. In 1593 Richard Craddock was so concerned at the quality of the services that he left money to pay a visiting clergyman to preach a sermon every Sunday morning. The old chapel of St Bertelin was now disused. Part of it was converted into a school-room and the rest into a room where the Council could meet. The town armour and weapons were hung round the walls.[5] In 1593, during a great storm, the spire of the church collapsed and 'beat down the church on every side'.[6] Repairs were carried out but the spire was not rebuilt.

Many older people regretted the passing of familiar Catholic services and, after his resignation as vicar, Thomas Cheddulton probably held services in private for some of them. As the political quarrel between England and Catholic Spain grew fiercer, Catholic priests, trained abroad, were smuggled into England, where they were hunted down as a political threat to the government. In 1588 one of these priests, Robert Sutton, was discovered at Stafford and hung, drawn and quartered. Local people did not see those local families who remained Catholic in private as a political threat. When government agents hunting another priest came to town in 1612, Thomas Worswick, the town clerk, kept

them drinking at his house while a warning was sent to local Catholics.[7] In the 1640s there were said to be 40 Catholics in the town who did not attend services in the parish churches.

During the Commonwealth, the Church of England was dismantled in favour of a Presbyterian church enforcing a strict puritanical code. In Stafford, Daniel Bayley, the Rector of St Mary's was put out of his church but the Corporation failed to appoint a successor for several years. Later, there was a growth of independent, self-governing protestant groups in the town. Most numerous were the Baptists who included Colonel Danvers, the military governor of the town, in their number.[8]

In 1660, with the restoration of Charles II, came the restoration of the Church of England as a national church. The old ministers, like Daniel Bayley, returned and the new were ejected. The Corporation Act made all who refused to take the sacrament according to the rites of the Anglican Church into second-class citizens. They were barred from municipal corporations, Parliament, universities, the army and navy, and teaching. In 1689, the Test Act gave most Protestants the right to build chapels and appoint their own minister, although they remained barred from positions of power. Between 1660 and 1689 there was a struggle between those who wanted toleration of different beliefs and those who wanted to persecute religious minorities, both Catholic and Protestant. The people and Corporation of Stafford preferred to be tolerant as long as minorities pursued their religion quietly. Although there were occasions when feelings ran high.

When Daniel Bayley was restored as Rector of St Mary's, the Baptists and Presbyterians continued to meet in private houses. The Baptists rapidly dwindled in number and nothing more is known of them. The Presbyterians continued to attend the parish church as well as meeting at Widow Slade's house. In 1689 they built a chapel in Balk Passage, off Mount Street, almost hidden in Sarah Salte's garden. Their first treasurer was John Dancer, an alderman who later became

108 *Right.* The original Presbyterian chapel built in 1674.

109 *Below right.* Until 1874 St Chad's Church was hemmed in by shops and could only be reached through an archway from Greengate Street. The tower, which was repaired in 1740, can be seen over the shops.

mayor. In 1715, during riots against dissenters, the chapel was damaged and its doors and pews burnt in the market place. By the mid-18th century the congregation was confined to a few families of Scottish descent.[9]

Quakers, who refused to take the oath of allegiance and made themselves noticeable, were always likely to be persecuted. In 1654 Miles Bateman 'declared in the streets of Stafford' and was whipped and imprisoned by order of the mayor. In the 1660s, Thomas Taylor was put in gaol, but continued to preach from the windows of the gaol. Quakers refused to be buried in St Mary's churchyard and bought a small piece of land in Foregate as a burial ground. An adjoining house became a meeting house, and those attending were at times imprisoned. In 1685 the mayor ordered the doors to be barred but the congregation continued to meet in the street outside. Persecution went on until 1696, when affirmation was accepted instead of an oath on the Bible.[10]

In the late 17th century Catholics were still liable to a range of penalties but were generally left in peace. The Fowler family at St Thomas', two miles out of town, kept a Catholic priest who celebrated mass in private houses in the town. When James II became king and allowed them freedom of worship, a chapel was opened in the town but, when James fled abroad and feeling against Catholics was running high, this was destroyed by a mob.[11]

During the 18th century churchgoing in Stafford became a habit rather than a matter of religious conviction for many families. Congregations declined; buildings were neglected. Nonconformity almost withered away. After visiting Stafford, John Wesley wrote, 'There are few towns in England less infected with religion'.

St Chad's had always been a poor church. There was no money for repairs and by 1740 the building was so neglected that the west end collapsed. The church was then encased in brick with iron-framed windows and the interior plastered to hide any remaining Norman features. Money was donated from outside the parish but the church bells had to be sold to complete the repairs.[12] Only one service of afternoon prayers and a sermon was held each month and the curate made up his salary by holding another post, such as vicar of Castlechurch or usher at the grammar school, in plurality.

St Mary's also deteriorated. The chancel was used only once a month for communion services and the nave was filled with privately owned high-sided box pews. There were galleries on three sides and a pulpit in front of the west gallery. In 1777 the church had to be closed for urgent repairs and in 1801 the old St Bertelin's Chapel was pulled down. By the 1830s the south wall of the chancel leaned outwards and the piers that supported the tower were crumbling. In the words of a guide book, 'It would be beautiful as a ruin, but as a place of worship it is disgraceful'.[13]

Eighteenth-century nonconformity was in no better state. By the end of the century the Presbyterians were reduced to three or four people holding a Sunday prayer meeting. The Quakers, reduced to two families by 1751, had no meetings for several years in the 1770s. The Congregational church, formed after James Boden of Hanley had preached in Market Square, built a meeting house with money provided by Lady Glenorchy in 1792. By 1803 it had only seven members.

John Wesley himself visited the town and preached here in the 1780s. His attempt to 'plant a grain of mustard seed that may grow into a great tree' had an immediate, but short-lived, success. A Methodist society was formed in 1783 and a chapel opened in 1785. By 1796 the society was disbanded. The disused chapel was sold in 1802.

As in other towns religious conviction revived in Stafford in the 19th century. There was a steady growth of Nonconformist churches, supported particularly by the working classes, and an expansion of church provision of all kinds in newly populous areas. A religious census held one Sunday in 1851[14] showed that more than half the adults in the town had attended church that day. Thirty-two per cent were at Non-conformist and eight per cent at Catholic churches but an overwhelming 60 per cent were at Anglican churches in the town. This was unusual in a town with a substantial part of the population engaged in industry.

Catholic resurgence was the earliest. From about 1780 a priest was living in the town and by 1791 a priest's house and chapel dedicated to St Austin had been built on the Wolverhampton Road. By 1817 this was too small and the Jerninghams of Stafford Castle paid for a larger church on the same site. By 1857 the church was 'crammed morning and evening' and money was raised for a third St Austin's Church, opened in 1862 and substantially the church to be seen today. At the opposite end of the town a mass centre was opened at St Patrick's Roman Catholic School in 1884 and a church behind the school in 1895.

In 1830 the Presbyterians appointed their first resident minister since the mid-18th century. A revival followed and the chapel was enlarged in 1835. Three years later the congregation split, with the majority following their minister, Alexander Stewart, into the Brethren movement. Their meeting room, opened in 1839, still exists on the corner of Church Lane. By 1851 the Presbyterian congregation had recovered and numbered over 150 people. In 1901 the chapel was enlarged and the south end rebuilt with a tower.[15]

The Congregationalists built Zion Chapel in Martin Street in 1811 on an over ambitious scale to seat 750. Half the congregation seceded in 1857 to form a Baptist church and other secessions followed. The seceding Baptists met at a room in Eastgate Street and then at the Lyceum Theatre, before building a chapel in Water Street. As the congregation increased, a larger chapel was built on The Green in 1896 with an eye-catching open tracery stone spire.[16]

After its false start in the late 18th century, Wesleyan Methodism was re-established in the town about 1805 and grew rapidly. The first

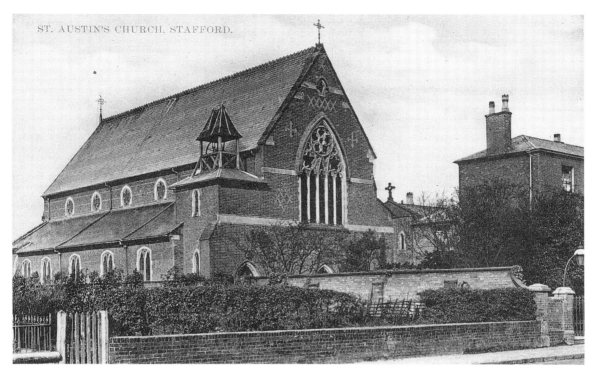

ST. AUSTIN'S CHURCH, STAFFORD.

110 St Austin's Roman Catholic Church in 1905. The priest's house, seen on the right of the picture, dates from 1791 and part of the original church of the same date can be seen behind it. The later church was consecrated in 1862 but the planned tower and spire were replaced by a turret and bell to reduce the cost.

111 The Zion Chapel in Martin Street was built by the Congregationalists in 1812 with a plain brick front. The ornate façade, seen in this photograph, incorporated the massive four-columned portico removed from the General Infirmary and was added in 1897.

112 The Baptist Chapel on the Green, with its distinctive open tracery stone spire designed by Ewen Harper, was opened in 1896. In this 1904 view Lockett's ginger-beer and mineral-water factory can be seen to the right of the chapel.

113 Three Wesleyan Methodist chapels: the 1785 'room' was sold in 1802 and then converted into a cottage; the chapel built in 1812; and the larger chapel built on the same site in 1864 and used until the 1980s.

chapel was opened in Chapel Street in 1812. By 1851 congregations numbered over 200 and a larger chapel with a tower was built on the site in 1864. A Sunday school/chapel was opened in Rowley Street in 1886 and a separate chapel to serve the north end of the town in 1909. The Methodist New Connection built a chapel in County Road in 1817 and, later on, a larger one in Gaol Square, which seated 500 people and often had 200 adults and as many Sunday school pupils at its services. The Primitive Methodists also built a chapel seating 300 at the south end of Gaol Road in 1849.[17]

St Mary's was both parish and civic church. Joseph Dickenson and his son, both dignified high churchmen, were rectors for 76 years from 1745 to 1821 and under them the church slumbered and the Corporation took all fees,

appointed both churchwardens, and proclaimed there was no money to repair the church. In 1822 the new rector was W.E. Coldwell, a young evangelical clergyman, who rapidly asserted his rights and chafed that he could do little to save the church from collapse. A survey by George Gilbert Scott, the architect, had shown the urgency of repair but an appeal launched by the rector met with a pathetic response.

When Jesse Watts Russell of Ilam Hall offered £5,000 to renew the interior of a church, a successful claim was made on behalf of St Mary's and a renewed appeal was more successful in raising money for rebuilding. George Gilbert Scott was entrusted with the work.

Scott had to stabilise the tower whose piers were crumbling. He also rebuilt the south transept and the south wall of the chancel as he thought

114   St Mary's Church before restoration.

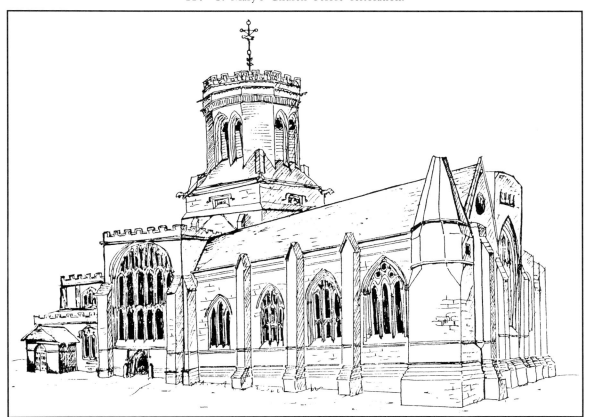

115 St Mary's Church after restoration.

116 The south chancel aisle of St Mary's was rebuilt by G.G. Scott between 1842 and 1844. This print, from John Masfen's *Views of the Church of St Mary at Stafford* (1852), shows the rebuilt aisle.

they would have been in the 13th century. Even greater changes were made to the interior. Galleries and box pews were swept away, the chancel opened up, and the altar turned into the focus for worship. Colourful wall tiles, a stained-glass window donated by Jesse Watts Russell himself and a crimson velvet altar cloth embroidered by his daughters provided a setting for what must have seemed a revolution in church services.[18]

By the mid-19th century St Chad's was in more regular use, with morning and afternoon services every Sunday. The church was also in need of repair. When work began in 1854 it was quickly realised that much of the original Norman church survived under the interior plaster and brick shell. Over the next 32 years this was slowly revealed and restored. A new west front was built in Norman style. Since the 17th century the church had been approached by an entry between shops in Greengate Street. These were taken down to open up a view of the restored building.

117 The interior of St Chad's Church after 1744 with walls plastered over and winged cherubs added near the roof. The chancel arch has been boxed in and plastered so that none of its Norman feature remains visible.

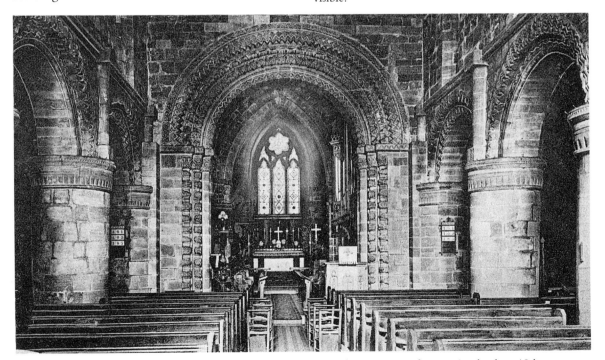

118 The interior of St Chad's Church after the restoration of its Norman features in the late 19th century.

The Anglican church was very active in 19th-century Stafford. As the town expanded, new churches were built to serve the newly populous areas.[19] Christ Church, serving the northern suburbs, was opened in 1839—with less formal services than St Mary's. By 1851 it was attracting congregations of 450 and by 1902 had its own mission church, St Aidan's. At Littleworth, St John the Baptist mission centre opened in 1886, although a separate parish and church did not follow until 1928. Services were also held at Broadeye School from 1878 until nearby St Bertelin's Church was opened in 1900. All these were in what was originally St Mary's parish.

New churches were also opened in Castlechurch parish. St Paul's, on the Lichfield Road, opened in 1844 and rapidly established a working partnership with St Chad's. From St Paul's a mission church and school at Rickerscote was established in 1877. In the railway suburb of Castletown, a much needed church was built in 1866 through the generosity of James Tyrer of Tixall, a major shareholder in the London North Western Railway. All the sittings were free and William Kendall, the first incumbent, was such a charismatic preacher that his church was often packed with 'fine silks and satins who, like cuckoos, pushed the railway workers out of their own church'.

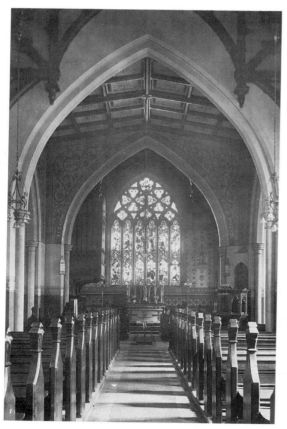

119 *Above left*. The interior of St Paul's Church, *c.*1914, shortly before the poppy heads of the pew ends were cut off because the vicar claimed they obscured the congregation's view of services.

120 *Above right*. St Thomas' Church, Castletown, a building in early English style designed by W. Culshaw of Liverpool for James Tyrer of Tixall in 1866. The Staffordshire Newsletter offices now occupy the site.

121 The interior of Christ Church, *c*.1918, showing the chancel screen erected in 1909. The vicar at that time was the Rev. J.E. Jones, a well-known Evangelical preacher.

Nonconformist, Catholic and Anglican churches all continued to attract numerous townspeople until the 1920s. From that time, although the population of the town continued to grow, attendance at churches and chapels began to decline.

There was a strong Anglo-Catholic movement in the town. This was strengthened in 1923 when Rev. William Shawcross, newly installed as vicar of Christ Church, announced: 'I shall lead the parish on Catholic lines. The most marked outward change will be the introduction of incense, which we shall begin on Ascension Day.' He went on to make it clear that he was to be called 'Father' and that Holy Communion would in future be referred to as the 'Mass'.

At St Mary's, the Rev. Lionel Lambert organised a 1,000-signature petition against the 1928 revision of the Prayer Book and then proclaimed that, as rector of a Royal Free Church, he was not subject to any directions or visitation from the bishop. The bishop took him to court, and in 1929 obtained a ruling that St Mary's ceased to be a Royal Free Church at the time of Queen Elizabeth's grant to the town of 1571.

In the years after the Second World War, some churches were forced to close because of declining congregations and rising costs. The large Congregational chapel in Martin Street was sold to the County Council and replaced by a more modest building in Eastgate Street. Methodists, who had accepted the principle of amalgamation in the 1930s, closed the New Connection chapel

122 The Wesleyan Methodists opened a school chapel in Rowley Street in 1885. It was built back from the road to allow a chapel to be built in front of it, but no chapel was built until 1909, the year before this postcard was published.

soon after the war, and the Primitive Methodist chapel in 1958. Worship was concentrated on the chapels in Mount Street and Rowley Street. In the 1980s, the Mount Street site was required for the new St John's Market and the chapel was rebuilt as the Trinity Methodist and United Reformed Church.

The Anglicans also shed some of their churches. In Castletown, St Thomas' was declared redundant in 1972 and amalgamated with St Andrew's at Doxey. In Foregate, Christ Church, suffering from 'an unreliable heater, a steady decline in numbers at services to almost nothing, and the redevelopment of the Gaol Square area', closed in 1976, leaving a minister with no church base, until Rowley Street Methodists offered to share their building. In the town centre, St Chad's and St Mary's were united as a single parish in 1973.

To balance these closures money has been raised for new churches in newly built-up areas. The Anglicans at Holmcroft were raising money

under the Bishop's 'New Churches and Men to man them' Appeal in the 1930s but the new church of St Bertelin was not consecrated until 1956. St Peter's Church at Rickerscote was opened in 1957, and a new church at Doxey for the combined parishes of St Thomas and St Andrew in 1975. There are also new non-conformist churches or church halls at Rising Brook and Holmcroft.

The Catholic church completed the rebuilding of St Patrick's with the opening of a new church there in 1963. A mass centre for the Weeping Cross area was started at Leasowes School in 1963; it moved to a church/hall dedicated to St Anne in 1966 and became a separate church in 1986. A mass centre opened at Bower Norris School in the late 1960s has closed and plans for a church in the area have been abandoned.

Money has also been found to refurbish older buildings. St Austin's was extensively restored to mark its bicentenary in 1991. St Mary's churchyard

123 An aerial view of St Mary's in 1957. On the right are the schools designed by G.G. Scott in 1856.

124 An informal Easter service at St Peter's, Rickerscote, in the early 1980s. The pews and much of the furniture for this modern church were made by craftsmen from the English Electric Company which then donated them to the church.

has had its gravestones removed to the sides and the site laid out as a Garden of Remembrance. Also at St Mary's, a new altar under the tower crossing has brought the congregation and officiating clergy closer to each other. Many other churches have raised money for interior refurbishment and modernisation.

Church services are changing. Many churches are attempting to make services less remote and more attractive to young people and families. At an ecumenical service held at St Austin's in 1987 there was 'dancing in the aisles'. Not all churchgoers have welcomed the changes. In his history of St Paul's, Forebridge,

Fred Imm records the shock when a new vicar told the congregation that he was not to be addressed as 'Vicar' but as 'Eric'.

Churches have also come together. In 1980 St Mary's, St Chad's, St Bertelin's and Christ Church parishes united and are now served by a team ministry. In 1985 the Methodist Conference at Birmingham recognised the Anglican vicar at Rowley Street as a Methodist minister working alongside the Rowley Street minister. United services became a regular feature of the church. The Stafford Council of Churches represents all denominations and has arranged a number of ecumenical missions and services in the town.

CHAPTER EIGHT

Schools

The Dean and College had maintained a school at St Mary's until they were abolished in 1548. Afterwards, the school continued with Humphrey Peckeman, one of the chantry priests, as master. The school endowment was small and the school-room was among the property confiscated by the Crown. The Corporation petitioned the king for a more adequate endowment and in 1550 the Free Grammar School of King Edward VI was established with £20 a year paid out of the rents of confiscated lands.[1] The Corporation were to appoint the master and usher, or second master, and draw up rules for the school with the advice of the Bishop of Coventry and Lichfield.

In 1571, when Queen Elizabeth I granted much of the confiscated land to the Corporation, they became responsible for paying £20 a year for the salaries of master and usher and maintenance of the building. They made the old St Bertelin's Chapel available as a school-room and paid for improvements, like boarding underfoot the low aisle 'for more wholesomeness for the children'. They also allowed the master to take out-of-town children into the school for a small weekly fee, which he kept. By 1600 the school had boarders from several well-to-do county families.

Pupils had to be able to read and write before they were admitted. At first they would be taught by the usher; later, the best pupils would be transferred to the master's class. Town boys paid no fees but had to buy their own books and pay for firing. Poor families could not afford to send their children to the school. All that was done was centred round Latin. The pupils wrote Latin, translated Latin books and even spoke Latin if they became good enough scholars. A few older pupils also learned Greek.

Morning school was from 7.00 a.m. to 11.00 a.m. and afternoon school from 1.00 p.m. to 5.00 p.m. or dusk in winter. The day began with morning prayers and an Old Testament reading and ended with evening prayers and a New Testament reading. On Sundays all the scholars went in a body to church, where a special place was reserved for them.[2] In 1636 a complaint was made that, because the master did not sit with his pupils, they 'do game at time of Divine Service'.[3] At school, special care was taken 'for the good manners and decent deportment of the Scholars'. 'Disobedient and stubborn youths' were expelled after one warning to their parents. Lesser offences like 'notching desks', breaking windows or 'abusing books' were to be met with unspecified 'exemplary punishment'.

The school curriculum changed little. By the 18th century the tradesmen of the town wanted their sons educated in English, mathematics, book-keeping and science not Latin. The number of pupils declined. The school's income failed to keep pace with rising costs and an ageing building. In 1713 the scholars paid for the chimney to be rebuilt. Salaries paid to the master and usher were inadequate to attract good teachers. At one time the usher, the Rev. John Wright, lived in Newcastle and rode to school only when he felt like it. He ignored all demands for his resignation. In 1749 the Corporation lamented that the grammar school has 'been neglected for some time past to the great detriment of the town'.[4]

A change took place with the appointment of the Rev. Joseph Shaw as master in 1780. He stayed for 45 years and took note of what the better class tradesmen wanted for their children. He introduced additional subjects like French, writing, and drawing for a small additional fee. The Rev. Joseph Ellerton, appointed usher in 1796, was to teach writing and accounts for no more than three shillings a quarter. The school curriculum was directed chiefly to English grammar, writing and arithmetic as 'not a sixth part of the boys ever wish to learn the classics, being principally destined for commerce and manufactures'. By 1824 the Charity Commission reported that the school was hardly a grammar school.

In 1801 the Corporation decided that, as the school-room was in poor repair and space was needed to extend the churchyard, the building should be taken down and the materials used to build a new school on the site of the old gaol near the Northgate. The new building was ill adapted to a school and it too was taken down

in 1813. The materials were again reused for a new school-room at the Gaol Square end of North Walls.

When Shaw died in 1825 the Corporation, after some disagreement, appointed as master the Rev. George Norman, curate at St Mary's. Norman refused to teach anything except classics, with the result that the number of pupils fell from over 100 to fewer than 20 pupils.

In 1835 the Municipal Corporation Act transferred responsibility for running the grammar school to trustees under the Charity Commission. Appointment of a third 'English' master, whose salary was to be paid out of fees charged to his pupils, was sanctioned against Norman's bitter opposition. By 1843 Norman and the usher were teaching the four remaining classical students between them and the 'English' master had been ejected from the school building.

The grammar school provided no education for children who started work at an early age. In Gloucester, Robert Raikes had begun Sunday schools for these children and the idea spread. In

125   King Edward VI Grammar School in North Walls in 1837.

126 The National School in Gaol Road in 1843. The school closed in 1909 but was not demolished until the 1980s. The foundation stone is preserved in the wall adjoining the Beth Johnson Home in Foregate Court.

1805 William Jones, a 21-year-old Methodist, who had experience of the Sunday school at Burslem, opened the first Sunday school in Stafford, in a room used by the Methodists in St Chad's Place. Within four months, the original 30 children had grown to 250 and the Sunday school had to move to the Assembly Room at the Shire Hall. Children were taught to read from the Bible and those who attended regularly and behaved well could go on to learn to write. Jones was soon joined by other teachers, while subscribers paid for quills, books and rent of the room.

Supporters and children were of all religious denominations but after Sunday school they all attended a service at St Mary's. When the new Wesleyan Methodist chapel opened in 1811 this was objected to and in 1812 the Sunday school divided. An Anglican school met in the chancel of St Mary's and a Methodist school in the new chapel. Other chapels started their own Sunday schools. In 1855, to mark the jubilee of the first Sunday school in the town, 500 Nonconformist pupils were each given a medal and a treat of cake and wine in the Shire Hall. The Anglican Sunday schools at St Mary's and St Chad's declined to take part.[5]

At the beginning of the 19th century, elementary education was the responsibility of church and charity not government. Charitable societies might make grants towards building costs but a church congregation had to struggle to raise money to build and maintain a school. Every pupil had to bring two or three pence a week towards the master's salary, coals for the fire and books.

The first elementary school in Stafford was built for St Austin's Catholic Church by Sir George Jerningham of Stafford Castle and a Mrs. Frith in 1818.[6] This was followed, in 1825, by two schools with grants from the Church of England's National Society for Promoting the Education of the Poor in the Principles of the Established Church. The National School in Gaol Road was built by St Mary's but later transferred to Christ Church.[7] Forebridge National School, built with help from Bridgeman's charity, replaced an older, smaller charity school. In 1842 it became St Paul's National School.[8]

127   Girls from the British School in Earl Street with their teachers, *c.*1890. They all seem to have worn their best clothes for the photographer.

The Nonconformists in Stafford had difficulty raising money for day schools although they had flourishing Sunday schools. In 1843 a British School was opened in Earl Street with help from the British and Foreign School Society and Mrs. Birch, a wealthy Methodist. Seven years later, the Methodist New Connection opened a school on the ground floor of their Gaol Square chapel. Both closed for lack of funds in the 1850s although the British School reopened in 1862.[9]

As the population of the town grew, both Anglicans and Catholics extended their schools and opened new ones. St Mary's National School opposite the church was opened in 1856, St Thomas' National School in Castletown in 1863, Eastgate National School in 1863, and St Mary's National School in Broadeye in 1868. The Catholics also opened a new school at the corner of Foregate and St Patrick's Street.

All these were large, single rooms where a master kept order over large numbers of children, while he and a group of older pupils (called pupil-teachers) taught smaller groups. The larger schools separated boys from girls and infants with a mistress in charge. Standards were understandably low, books and equipment in short supply and attendance erratic.

In 1863 the government, which had been making annual grants to some schools for several years, decided to make grants only if the schools were efficient. In future, school managers would only be able to apply for a grant if there was a qualified teacher in charge and buildings and equipment reached approved standards. The amount of grant was decided by an annual inspection and test of the three Rs. Every pupil earned a grant for regular attendance and for each test passed. The system, known as Payment by

Results, was rigid and unpopular but it did raise standards in schools.

Conditions in schools can be judged by the following report on Rowley Street School which had a single room 53 ft. by 27 ft. and a master, Mr. Coppard, assisted by a young lad.

In the first standard there are 90 children all taught in one class under one teacher ... in the second standard 75 ... The length of the room makes it impossible for Mr. Coppard to have proper superintendence and the echo increases the difficulty.[10]

Meanwhile dissatisfaction with the grammar school's classical education had led to the appointment of new trustees and the introduction of an English/commercial curriculum which ran parallel to the classics and was funded by charging fees for all pupils. There were further changes after the retirement of the Rev. Norman.

In 1862 the school moved to new purpose-built premises on Newport Road, with an adjoining house for the headmaster. In 1873, when a revised scheme brought in local governors, there was a commercial class for pupils aged eight to 14 and a classical class for those from 10 to 16 years of age. Fees were relatively high and the education provided for most pupils was no more advanced than in a good elementary school. Numbers remained low until the end of the century, but the reputation of the school in the town grew and opportunities for more advanced studies for the best pupils increased.[11]

By this time, the government had decided to introduce state elementary schools. The Education Act of 1870 provided for a locally elected school board which could build schools wherever there was a shortage of school places and maintain them by levying a local rate on all

128 King Edward VI Grammar School, Newport Road, 1904. The headmaster's house is on the left. The single storey part of the building was given an upper storey in 1905.

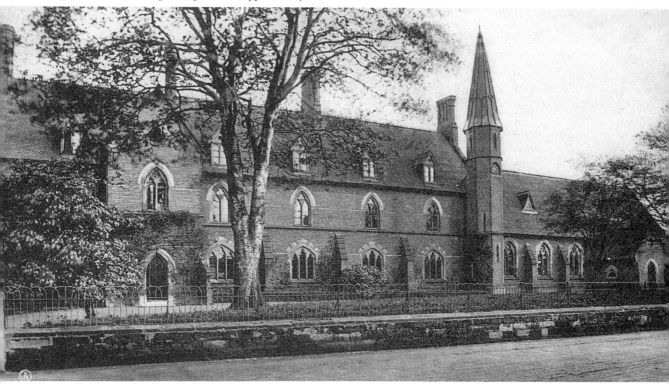

129   King Edward VI Grammar School pupils in 1871. The headmaster at the time was Rev. Charles Uppleby Bower, seen here on the left. He was also vicar of St Chad's.

130   Corporation Street School was extended in 1909 when it was divided into separate boys', girls' and infants' schools. This is the girls' school in 1910. The buildings were damaged by brine subsidence in the 1960s and extensively rebuilt.

131 This faded photograph shows the pupils of North Street Infants' School posed in their classroom in the early 1920s.

householders. In Stafford, there was already extensive school provision by the Church of England, who also planned to build a new boys' school in Rowley Street and turn Christ Church School into a girls-only school, and by the Catholics. The British School was the only one maintained by the Nonconformists. A count taken in 1870 showed 909 pupils at Anglican schools, 350 at Catholic schools and 222 at the British School. A total of 400 pupils on school books were absent on the day when the count was taken.[12]

With this number of places, a school board was unnecessary in the town, but the Church of England clergy campaigned for one to be elected because this was the only way schooling could be made compulsory. In December 1870 the Town Council agreed in order to 'compel attendance of those children who now run about the streets acquiring bad habits'.[13] The first school board of nine members included one Catholic and five Anglican clergymen. Education was made com-

pulsory from the age of five to 13, with exemption for pupils over the age of 10 who reached a specified standard. This was strongly rejected by Nonconformists who complained that their children would be foreced to attend Church of England schools.

The British School was always in financial difficulty. In 1877, as a result of a bad report by visiting H.M. Inspectors, it lost half its government grant. Some improvements were made but in 1894 the Nonconformist governors, having insufficient money to maintain the building and pay its teachers, handed the school over to the School Board. It was replaced by a new school in Corporation Street, built and maintained out of a local rate.[14]

Standards rose slowly as government inspectors demanded better buildings, more equipment, and higher standards of work. Schools were encouraged to earn additional government grants by widening the curriculum. In the 1890s they were given greater freedom when grants were

132 *Left*. The Stafford Technical School, built in 1896, provided offices for the County Technical Committee. In 1903 these were taken over by the new County Education Department and the building was extended along Earl Street.

133 *Below left*. Physical training in the yard at Rowley Street Boys' School about 1907.

134 *Below*. St Paul's National School football team in 1905-6, photographed with the headmaster, Mr. C.J. Henry.

based on an annual report on the school instead of on tests given to every pupil. In 1896, for example, Christ Church Girls' School replaced plain needlework for the younger pupils with cork work, button-holing, embroidery, drawing, colouring and paper folding.[15] H.M. Inspector Parez thought the changes had made schools 'a sort of fairyland instead of an ergasterium'.[16]

By 1900 pupil teachers were being replaced by trained assistant teachers and large school-rooms were divided into class rooms. The cost of these changes and the increasing cost of books and equipment for a broader curriculum caused a crisis in many church schools which were financed from money raised by their congregations.

The 1902 Education Act made sweeping changes. School boards were abolished and borough and county councils took over all their school buildings. They also assumed responsibility for day-to-day costs, including salaries and equipment, in all elementary schools. The managers of church schools kept responsibility for maintaining their own buildings and for deciding how religious education should be taught in their schools. In Stafford, the Borough Council decided to surrender all its educational responsibilities to the County Council.

The new system was angrily opposed by some Nonconformists who objected to paying rates which went towards the support of Anglican and Catholic schools. In Stafford, the Primitive Methodists led the opposition and helped to form a branch of the League of Passive Resistance which refused to pay a proportion of local rates. Opposition continued for several years.[17]

Since 1902 the development of schools in Stafford has been a reflection of the policies of the County Education Committee. There is no space here to do more than note a few of its more prominent features.

In the years before 1914 the County Council built a new school in St Leonard's Avenue, largely to cope with families from the new Siemen's factory, extended Corporation Street School to allow Christ Church National

135 St Leonard's School, opened in 1906 to replace temporary classes in the Baptist chapel, was built mainly to provide education for the children whose families moved to Stafford with Siemen Bros.

136 Pupils of St Mary's, Littleworth, photographed outside their school in 1914. The school was renamed St John's, *c.*1923.

137 The chemistry laboratory added to King Edward VI Grammar School as part of the extensions in 1928 and photographed soon afterwards.

School to be closed, and built a school in Tenterbanks to replace the National School at Broadeye and the girls' department of St Mary's National School.[18] The closure of these obsolete school buildings substantially reduced the dominant place of Church of England schools in the town.

It was not until the early 20th century that the idea of elementary and grammar schools as steps on the same educational ladder was accepted. The County Education Committee provided scholarships 'to enable and induce children to pass from the elementary school to the secondary school', and the Board of Education offered

government grants to grammar schools on condition that 25 per cent of places were offered free to pupils from elementary schools.[19] Numbers in grammar schools rose and more pupils stayed on to 16 or even 18 years of age. By 1919 King Edward VI Grammar School had 210 boys, the buildings were overcrowded and there was no money for repairs or extensions. In the following year, the Education Committee agreed to take over the school and by 1928 had built a new hall and wing along Friars Terrace. There was no parallel school for girls until 1907 when the Education Committee took over a private school, opened at the Moat House in 1903, and rehoused

138 The Girls' High School moved into this building at The Oval in 1907, shortly before this picture was taken. The girls in the foreground may be pupils but the other children were simply collected and posed by the photographer.

139 Girls' High School pupils photographed at The Oval about 1930 when gymslips were a universal uniform.

140 Boys from St Patrick's Roman Catholic School, wearing red and blue sashes, are lined up outside the school to take part in the procession in honour of Our Lady in May 1923.

141 Riverway Senior Girls' School was opened in 1939, became a secondary modern school after the 1944 Education Act, and a middle school for pupils aged 9 to 13 in 1976. About 1990 it was taken over by the County Highways Department and renamed Highway House.

it in new buildings at The Oval. Fees were still charged but free places and scholarships were offered, as at King Edward VI School.

The school leaving age was raised to 14 by the 1918 Education Act, which also required education committees to draw up plans to provide a wider and more practical education for all senior pupils not attending grammar schools. A government report in 1926 went further and recommended that in future schools should be divided into primary (ages five to 11) and secondary (over 11). In Stafford, some progress was made in replacing old buildings and classes over 50 were eliminated, but there was no progress towards new secondary modern schools until 1929 when government building grants, offered for three years, led to frantic activity. The national financial crisis in 1931 halted grants for new

buildings, cut the grant for books to 5s. per pupil and brought an end to plans to move all pupils over 11 to secondary modern schools by 1932.[20]

It was not until 1939 that Dartmouth Street Secondary Modern Boys' and Riverway Secondary Modern Girls' Schools were opened. A third school at Rising Brook was unfinished when war broke out and was requisitioned by the Admiralty until the end of the Second World War.

After the war, Rising Brook was used as a temporary primary school until Highfields Primary School was opened in 1954. Both Anglicans and Catholics took advantage of the generous funding available under the 1944 Education Act to replace and extend their schools. The County Education Committee also opened no fewer than 15 new primary schools to serve estates on the edge of the town. Today the

142 Bower Norris Roman Catholic Primary School was one of many new schools opened after 1945. This photograph shows mass being celebrated by Bishop Terence Brain, a former parish priest at St Austin's, to mark its silver jubilee in July 1991.

majority of primary children are taught in post-war schools and class rooms.[21]

Fees in secondary grammar schools had been abolished by the 1944 Education Act and opinion was moving against the allocation of pupils to grammar or secondary modern schools at the age of eleven. The Education Committee favoured small comprehensive schools as the way forward in secondary education. The Department of Education was reluctant to approve. Trinity Fields Secondary Modern and Graham Balfour Grammar Schools were built as separate schools on the same site. The Girls' High School was also rehoused in new buildings off West Way where there was room for later expansion. The first of the new comprehensive schools was opened at Walton in 1967, followed by the amalgamation of Balfour and Trinity Fields Schools in 1968, and the extension of The Blessed William Howard Roman Catholic School into a comprehensive school in 1971. Meanwhile, the rest of the town retained its mixture of secondary modern and grammar schools.

This uneasy situation was resolved in 1975 when schools in the town, except in the Walton area, were re-organised into primary, middle and high schools. This paved the way for King Edward VI Boys' School and the Girls' High School to amalgamate and become a comprehensive. Rising Brook Secondary Modern School was also extended and became a comprehensive school.

By 1988, a falling child population and the resulting surplus of school places was resolved by reverting to primary and secondary schools, taking out of use some old primary accommodation and closing Kingston and Riverway Middle Schools. The old King Edward VI School building was converted in part into a sixth form centre.

Stafford also has a long tradition of private schools. Among the first were a boarding school for young ladies in Market Square in the 18th century and a commercial academy for boys in Eastgate Street in the 19th century. In post-war years this tradition has revived with Brooklands Preparatory School, opened in 1946 after the preparatory department at the Girls' High School closed, and Stafford Independent Grammar School, opened in 1982.

The Stafford Family

The Stafford family never lived in Stafford and, until recent boundary changes, Stafford Castle was not in the borough, yet their presence on the town's doorstep cannot be ignored.

The de Toeni family were hereditary standard bearers to the Dukes of Normandy. Robert de Toeni, a younger son of the family, invaded England with William the Conqueror and was rewarded with, among other lands, an estate consisting of several small hamlets south of Stafford. He was also given a considerable number of burgages in the town and the Earl of Mercia's share of the town's rent. On his estate he built a timber motte and bailey castle for the protection of himself and his Norman followers. Later, a village grew up at the castle gate and a church was built to serve the estate. Church and estate became known as Castlechurch and Robert took the name Robert of Stafford.

Robert and his descendants were not prominent among Norman barons.[1] They went about the job of managing their estate and developing it to increase their income, using the castle as both residence and administrative centre. The estate was without a mill so they bought the mill in Stafford, together with fishing rights in the Sow. Houses were built round the Green in Forebridge, just across the river from the borough. The Staffords had property in the borough but did not try to dominate it.

Robert had died in 1088. Eight generations later, in the 14th century, Ralph Stafford inherited estate and castle. He was an ambitious and able professional soldier who fought with distinction in Edward III's wars in Scotland and France and

was knighted for his services.[2] By 1337 he was Steward of the Royal Household and was chosen as one of the founding Knights of the Order of the Garter. In 1351 the king created him Earl of Stafford and gave him an annuity of 1,000 marks.

Ralph needed to support his position among the king's advisers. In 1348 he signed a contract with the mason John of Burcestre to rebuild the castle near Stafford in stone with a keep designed with memories of the castles he had seen in France.[3] He founded an Augustinian friary in Forebridge and made grants to the nearby St John's Hospital for masses to be said daily in its chapel. To pay for all this he needed money and, when his wife died, he carried off and married Margaret, the only child of Hugh Audley, whose fortune was many times greater than his own.

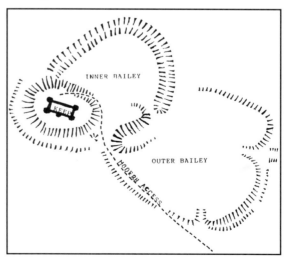

143 Plan of Stafford Castle showing the medieval keep and the earthworks round the two baileys.

When Ralph died in 1373 he was succeeded by his son Hugh, a deeply religious man and a member of the King's Council. Hugh was so distressed when his eldest son was killed in a brawl that he went on a pilgrimage to Jerusalem. He died at Rhodes on the way home.

His second and third sons died soon after their father, which meant that the youngest son, Edmund, inherited all the Stafford lands. He married Anne of Woodstock, daughter of the Earl of Gloucester and a close relation of the king as well as an heiress. The Staffords were now one of the great families of England with estates in many counties. Although they visited Stafford only occasionally, their influence in the borough grew through their estate officials. Significantly the earliest records of the borough courts are found among their estate papers.[4]

Edmund died leading the van of the king's army at the battle of Shrewsbury in 1403 and was buried in the church of the Austin Friars in Foregate. His widow was cousin to the king and reckoned to be the richest woman in England. Their son was created Duke of Buckingham. He was a member of the King's Council and Constable of France. His income was over £4,500 a year and his retinue splendid enough to provide the king's bodyguard at times.

His influence in Stafford borough must have been considerable. He had bought the right to appoint the dean of the Royal College and had founded a chantry in St Mary's Church. He was Recorder to the Borough and his household officers advised the bailiffs. They were also regularly chosen as M.P.s for the borough.[5] His coat of arms was even incorporated in the arms of the borough.[6] In later years, officers of his household were probably responsible for restricting the right of burgesses to choose the town bailiffs.

Humphrey was killed at the Battle of Northampton and his grandson and heir was brought up at court. There, he was involved in the intrigues of the Wars of the Roses, married the widowed mother of the future Henry VII, was beheaded and had his lands confiscated by Richard III. When Henry VII became king, he restored Buckingham's lands and titles to his son Edward. Edward built himself a magnificent castle at Thornbury, in Gloucestershire, and made so much of his royal lineage that he was seen as a potential threat to the king. In 1521 he was attainted, executed, and his lands and titles forfeited to the king.

By this time Stafford Castle had become little more than a hunting lodge. The main living quarters had been transferred to the bailey, where excavation has recovered 15th-century Venetian tableware as well as stirrups and fine metalwork from horses' harness.[7] The village outside the castle gates had been deserted and its site added to the deer parks which adjoined the castle.

In 1521, after it had been forfeited, it was reported that,

> this little castle ... should be right pleasant for the King when it shall please His Grace to make progress into these parts in the hunting season. The park having in it 400 deer.[8]

Stafford Castle was restored to Henry, Lord Stafford, in 1531 but most of the estates elsewhere were never returned. The family had lost its wealth and power. Stafford Castle was once more their main residence. In the town, the family's influence was undiminished. Property in the town had been recovered. Henry became Recorder of the Borough and both he and his son nominated most of the town's M.P.s. Queen Elizabeth even visited the castle in 1575.

Edward, Henry's son, resented his family's loss of status, comparing his 'rotten castle at Stafford' with the family's former home at Thornbury. He was forced to sell land to meet his expenses. His son, another Edward, is said to have married his mother's chamber maid. For a time he leased the castle but was living there again by the time he died in 1625.[9] His widow continued to live in the castle and during the Civil War it was 'Old Lady Stafford' who beat off a Parliamentary attack, but was later forced to withdraw in the face of overwhelming forces. In December 1643 the Parliamentary Committee at Stafford ordered the castle to be partly pulled down to make it uninhabitable and indefensible.[10]

144 Latin entry in Castlechurch parish register recording the burial of Lord Stafford in 1625.

The estate descended to Lady Stafford's granddaughter, who had married William Howard, third son of the Catholic Earl of Arundel. This ended the direct male line of the Staffords. In 1640 William was created Baron Stafford, a title which could be passed on through a woman, and later Viscount Stafford, a title which could not be passed on through a woman. During the Civil War his lands were confiscated by Parliament but restored by Charles II in 1660. He actively supported freedom for Catholics to worship without penalty, and in 1678 he was accused of plotting to make England a Catholic country. He was tried and executed in 1680, amid a frenzy of anti-Catholic feeling, but it was quickly realised that his accusers had lied and his property was restored to his son. In 1929 the Catholic church recognised that William had died a martyr for his religion and gave him the title Blessed William Howard.[11]

The Howards owned Stafford Castle and the land round it until the 1760s but had nothing to do with the town, apart from supporting its Catholic community. The daughter of the last Howard married Sir George Jerningham of Costessey in Norfolk.[12] The Jerninghams sheltered many exiled French Catholic nobles during the French Revolution and were prominent in the campaign to remove restrictions on Catholics worshipping freely and holding various public posts. They believed they could do this more effectively if they regained the title Lord Stafford, conferred in 1640 but extinguished by the attainder of William Howard in 1680.

Their claim would be strengthened by residence at Stafford Castle. The site had been no more than a tumble of stone when William Jerningham had cleared it and discovered that the basement storey was more or less intact. He had built up the walls to ten or twelve feet and planted several thousand trees with a walk said to be 'the Tonne of the Beau-monde from Stafford'. About 1811 Sir William's sons, Sir George and Edward, began to rebuild the castle on its old foundations. By 1817 'one front, flanked by two round towers in a very elegant castellated style', was complete and Edward was in residence.[13]

145 William Howard, Viscount Stafford.

146　Aerial view of Stafford Castle about 1945.

147　Most of the furniture was removed from the castle in the 19th century. This photograph of the hall, *c*.1920, shows the oak panelled walls with a frieze of sea horses. The iron crosses on the walls had once supported armour. The cases on the right held marble panels from the altar of Tixall Priory.

148 Stafford Castle in 1926. The message on the back of this postcard reads, 'Daddy went to Stafford to examine the police while Mother and I went over this castle. We went up a lot of worn steps to the top of the tower. In the foreground is the old chapel and a little to the right is the old dungeon with an chain'.

In 1824 Parliament annulled the attainder of William Howard on the grounds that he had been innocent of the charges. This enabled Sir George Jerningham to make a successful claim to the title Lord Stafford. Five years later most of the restrictions on Catholics were lifted.

The expense of rebuilding the castle was no longer seen as necessary and work stopped. After Edward Jerningham died a caretaker was put in to look after the building, and the walk through the woods to the castle once more became popular among the inhabitants of Stafford.

By 1949 cracks had appeared in the rebuilt east wall and the castle was declared unsafe. The caretaker moved out and vandals soon reduced the castle to a ruin. In 1961 Lord Stafford gave the site to Stafford Borough Council, who first demolished walls on the grounds that they were unsafe, and then, in 1978, began a programme of conservation and excavation with funding from the Manpower Services Commission.

Today the castle is open to the public. There is a visitors' centre at the foot of the motte and special events are held each year in the bailey. The land around the castle still belongs to Lord Stafford.

149 The Blazon Knights re-enact medieval times against the background of Stafford Castle in July 1996.

Notes

Abbreviations

Adey   -   Adey, K.R., *Aspects of the history of the town of Stafford 1590-1710*, unpublished M.A. thesis, Keele University, 1971

Higson   -   Higson, T.H., *Stafford Survey*, Stafford Borough Council, 1948

LHSB   -   Local History Source Books, published by the Staffordshire County Council Education Department

OSS   -   Transactions of the Old Stafford Society

Roxburgh   -   Roxburgh, A.L.P., *Know Your Town: Stafford*, Alison & Bowen, 1948

SA   -   Staffordshire Advertiser

SHC   -   Staffordshire Historical Collections. The early volumes published by the William Salt Archaeological Society and later volumes by the Staffordshire Record Society

SH&CS   -   Transactions of the Stafford Historical and Civic Society

SIAS   -   Transactions of the Staffordshire Industrial Archaeological Society

SRO   -   Staffordshire County Record Office

VCH   -   The Victoria County History of Staffordshire

WSL   -   The William Salt Library

Chapter One

1   Carver, M., *Underneath Stafford Town* (1979), The King's Pool

2   Darlington, J., *Stafford Past* (1994), p.23

3   Darlington, J., *Stafford Past* (1994), pp.22-3

4   Carver, M., *Underneath Stafford Town* (1979), Anglo-Saxon Stafford

5   LHSB L39, Lewis, R.A., *Three Stafford Churches* (1980), p.9

6   These excavations are reported in Oswald, A., *The Church of St Bertelin at Stafford and its Cross* (1955)

7   Stafford Borough Council, *Stafford Heritage Group News*, December 1994

8   *VCH*, vol. vi, p.199

9   *VCH*, vol. vi, p.235

10   *VCH*, vol. vi, pp.210-1

11   *VCH*, vol. vi, p.203

12   Midgley, L.M., 'Some Notes on Old Stafford and Old Staffordian's,' *SH&CS* 1974-6, pp.9-11

13   Bradley, J.W., *Royal Charters and Letters Patent Granted to the Burgesses of Stafford* (1897)

14   Stitt, F.B., 'Stafford Borough Court Rolls 1396-7', *SH&CS* 1974-6, pp.15-36

15   *VCH*, vol. iii, p.304

16   *VCH*, vol. vi, p.214

17   *VCH*, vol. vi, p.223

18   Wrottesley, Gen., *Subsidy Roll 1332*, SHC, vol. x, p.81; *VCH*, vol. vi, p.215

19   Midgley, L.M., *Some Staffordshire Poll Tax Returns*, SHC, Fourth Series, vol. vi, pp.l-16

20 'The Agreement with the Shoemakers of Stafford', *OSS*, 1936, pp.17-26

21 *Matthew Craddock; a short account of his connection with Stafford* (1979)

22 For Buckingham *see* Appendix, p.114

23 *VCH*, vol. vi, p.223

24 *VCH*, vol. vi, pp.222-3

25 Kettle, A.J., 'The Black Book of Stafford', *SH&CS*, 1965-7, pp.1-35

26 Cherry, J.L., *Stafford in Olden Times* (1890), p.71

Chapter Two

1 Kettle, A.J., *Matthew Craddock's Book of Remembrance 1614-5*, SHC, Fourth Series, vol. 16, pp.113-5

2 Legg, L.G. Wickham (Ed), *Relation of a Short Survey of 26 Counties*, p.55

3 WSL, *Copy of a lost plan of Stafford*. A date in the late 1620s is more probable than *c.*1600 suggested in *Transactions of the North Staffordshire Field Club*, vol. 58, p.56

4 Kidson, R., 'The Inhabitants of the Borough of Stafford 1622', *OSS*, 1956-9, pp.16-28

5 Kettle, A.J., *Matthew Craddock's Book of Remembrance 1614-5*, SHC, Fourth Series, vol. 16, pp.132-5

6 Stafford Borough Council, *Matthew Craddock, a short account of his connections with Stafford* (1979); for the family's overseas trade *see* Friis, A., *Alderman Cockayne's Project and the Cloth Trade* (1927), pp.282-6

7 Adey, p.181

8 Adey, pp.39-40

9 Adey, pp.41-3; SRO, D1721/1/4 ff114-5 & 134

10 Kettle, A.J., *Matthew Craddock's Book of Remembrance 1614-5*, SHC, Fourth Series, vol. 16

11 LHSB L7, Lewis, R.A., *Stafford in 1600* (1971), p.16

12 Butters, P., *Stafford: the Story of a Thousand Years* (1979), pp.46-8

13 Adey, pp.105-10

14 Kettle, A.J., *Matthew Craddock's Book of Remembrance 1614-5*, SHC, Fourth Series, vol. 16, p.74

15 LHSB L7, Lewis, R.A., *Stafford in 1600* (1971), pp.25-7 has a full account of James' visit

16 Adey, pp.30-8

17 WSL SMS 402, Mayor's Accounts, 1642; SRO D1323/E/1 f 260v

18 Hutton, R., *The Royalist War Effort 1642-6* (1982) pp.40-1

19 There is a contemporary account of the battle in SRO D868/2/69 and various modern accounts

20 *Mercurius Aulicus*, 25 May 1643

21 Pennington, D.H. and Rootes, I.A., *The Committee at Stafford, 1643-5*, SHC, Fourth Series, vol. 1

22 Cherry, J.L., *Stafford in Olden Times* (1890), p.56 quoting *The Perfect Diurnal*, 28 December 1646

23 Adey, pp.9-11; Rowlands, M. 'Houses and People in Stafford at the end of the 17th century', *OSS*, 1965-7, pp.46-56

24 Defoe, D., *A Tour through England and Wales* (Everyman edition) vol. 2, p.78

25 Adey, pp.115-6 & 139

26 Adey, p.112; *VCH*, vol. vi, p.209

27 Adey, chapter on Efficiency of Government, pp.74ff

28 'The Arrest of the Duke of Monmouth at Stafford 1682', *OSS* 1932 pp.21-9; 'William Feake', *OSS* 1934, pp.50-3

29   *VCH*, vol. vi, pp.237-8; Wedgwood, J.C., *Staffordshire Parliamentary History 1603-1780*, SHC 1920 and 1922

Chapter Three

1   S.R. and E., Broadbridge, 'Communication with Canals in the Stafford Area', *SIAS*, No. 1 (1970), pp.17-20
2   *VCH*, vol. vi, p.198
3   *VCH*, vol. vi, pp.197-8
4   *See* map in LHSB L2, Lewis, R.A., *Stafford Castle* (1959), p.26
5   Roxburgh, pp.101-2
6   WSL 26/38/22 and 'Autobiography of Whitworth', *OSS*, 1931, pp.27-37
7   Allbutt, M., 'Turnpike Roads of Stafford', *SIAS* No. 8 (1978) pp.7-8
8   *The Universal British Directory* (1793), Stafford; SA, 9 March 1805
9   White, W., *History, Gazetteer and Directory of Staffordshire* (1834) pp.152-3
10   Allbutt, M., 'Turnpike Roads of Stafford', *SIAS* No. 8 (1978), p.8
11   Roscoe, *Book of the Grand Junction Railway* (1839), p.61
12   SA, 8 July 1837
13   Gully, A.M., 'Historical Survey of the Railways serving Stafford', *SIAS* No. 8 (1978), pp.27-8
14   SRO D897/6
15   SA, 1 July 1837
16   SRO D897/6
17   SA, 1 July 1837
18   Calvert, C., *A History of Stafford and Guide to the Neighbourhood* (1886), pp.85-8
19   Talbot, E., *Railways in and around Stafford* (1994), p.8
20   Gully, A.M., 'Historical Survey of the Railways serving Stafford', *SIAS* No. 8 (1978), pp.21-4
21   SA, 14 July 1866
22   Gully, A.M., 'Historical Survey of the Railways serving Stafford', *SIAS* No. 8 (1978), pp.24-30
23   Talbot, E., *Railways in and around Stafford* (1994), pp.7-8
24   Gully, A.M., Historical Survery of the Railways serving Stafford, SIAS No. 8 (1978), p.37
25   SA, 23 November 1907
26   Higson, pp.22-4
27   *Stafford Newsletter*, 4 August 1962
28   *Stafford Newsletter*, 16 June 1978

Chapter Four

1   Adey, chapter on Trade and Occupations
2   OSS, 1932, pp.36-42: 1933, pp.53-61: 1934, pp.41-6: 1935, pp.53-7
3   Probate Inventory of James Godwyn, 8 June 1709
4   Horne, J.S., 'William Horton', *Staffordshire Life* (January 1953). The sources relating to his business are printed in LHSB L47, Lewis, R.A., *Stafford Shoes* (1984), pp.7-13
5   *Report of the Committee of the House of Commons into the effect of the proposed regulation about trade with Ireland* (1785); Evidence of William Horton
6   *The Universal British Directory of Trade, Commerce and Manufacture* (1793) under Stafford
7   LHSB L47, Lewis, R.A., *Stafford Shoes* (1984), pp. 18, 28
8   *Correspondence relative to the Introduction of Machinery into the Stafford Shoe Trade* (1855)

9   SA, 5 and 12 March 1859

10 *Report of the Children's Employment Commission: Shoe Manufacture* (1862); Evidence of Edwin Bostock

11 SA, 14 June 1924

12 *Business Jubilee of Frederick Riley Ltd.* (1931)

13 For David Hollin *see* LHSB L47, Lewis, R.A., *Stafford Shoes* (1984), pp.33-8

14 SA, 12 June and 26 December 1903: *VCH*, vol. vi, p.218

15 Higson, p.34

16 *Stafford Newsletter*, 7 June 1996

17 *VCH*, vol. vi, p.218; *Stafford Official Guide* (1950), pp.45-6

18 *Stafford: an Industrial Survey* (1932), pp.67-71

19 *VCH*, vol. vi, p.219

20 *VCH*, vol. vi, p.219

21 *Stafford: An Industrial Survey* (1932), p.75

22 Doubtfire, T., 'Henry Venables Ltd.', *SIAS* (1978), pp.43-9 and unpublished mss interview with Charles Venables

23 SA, *175th Anniversary Souvenir* (1970), p.55

24 SA, *175th Anniversary Souvenir* (1970), pp.18-19

25 Baker, A.C. and Civil, T.D.A., *Bagnalls of Stafford* (1973)

26 *VCH*, vol. vi, p.220

27 *VCH*, vol. ii, pp.157-9; *English Electric, Stafford* (c.1950); SA, *175th Anniversary Souvenir* (1970), p.41; Higson, pp.30-1

28 *Stafford: An Industrial Survey* (1932), pp.47-51; Imms, F., *St Paul's Forebridge Past and Present* (1995), pp.30-1

29 *VCH*, vol. ii, pp.250-1 and vol. vi, pp.221-2

Chapter Five

1   WSL 77/45 f55v

2   Powner, J.R., *A Duty Done* (1987), pp.28-32

3   WSL CB Stafford; SA, 15 September 1838

7   Cherry, J.L., *Stafford in Olden Times* (1890), p.83

8   *VCH*, vol. vi, p.225; White, W., *History, Gazetteer and Directory of Staffordshire* (1834), p.140

9   Williams, C., *The Staffordshire General Infirmary* (1992), pp.5-16

10 LHSB Study Book 1, Lewis, R.A., *Gaols* (1974), pp.7-14 and 37

11 White, W., *History, Gazetteer and Directory of Staffordshire* (1851), p.328

12 LHSB G17, Lewis, R.A., *Police in Staffordshire* (1974), p.14

13 *VCH*, vol. vi, p.226

14 SA, 4 and 11 March 1854

15 SA, 10 August 1867

16 Knight, E., *Report on the Sanitary State of Stafford* (1839)

17 SA, 23 July 1870

18 SRO D1323/A/1/6 p.200

19 SA, 6 September 1881

20 *VCH*, vol. vi, pp.232-3 for this paragraph

21 Powner, J.R., *A Duty Done* (1987), pp.81-2

22 *Stafford; an industrial survey* (1932), pp.31-2

23   Roxburgh, pp.17-18

24   'Stafford Gaol and the Easter Rising', *Picture Postcard Monthly*, July 1994, p.40

25   Lewis, R., *Stafford and District; a Portrait in Old Picture Postcards* (1991), p.29

Chapter Six

1   Roxburgh, pp.79-80

2   Job, H., *Staffordshire Windmills* (1985), pp.36-7

3   Skine, H., *Three Successive Tours in the North of England* (1795), p.2; Andrews, C.B. (ed.), *Torrington Diaries*, vol. 3, pp.135-6

4   Johnson, D.A., *Joshua Drewry*, SHC, Fourth Series, vol. 6, p.195

5   *VCH*, vol. ii, pp.364-7

6   Butters, P., *Stafford: the Story of a Thousand Years* (1979), pp.50-3

7   White, W., *History, Gazetteer and Directory of Staffordshire* (1834), p.109

8   Borrow, G., *Romany Rye* quoted by Roxburgh, p.25

9   LHSB L37, Lewis, R.A., *Old Stafford* (1979), p.5

10   Anslow, J., *St Thomas' Church, Castletown, Stafford* (1971), pp.5-7

11   SA, 20 December 1873

12   SA, 3 April 1875

13   SA, 24 March 1866

14   *Stafford Land Building & Improvement Co Ltd.; Plan of Rowley Hall Estate laid out in Building Plots.* (n.d.)

15   Calvert, C., *History of Stafford and Guide to the Neighbourhood* (1886), p.81

16   *Representation of the Mayor, Aldermen and Burgesses of Stafford to the Local Government Board as to the alteration of the boundary of the Borough* (1914), p.14

17   LHSB L40, Lewis, R.A., *Stafford Remembered* (1982), p.34

18   *VCH*, vol. vi, p.193

19   LHSB L40, Lewis, R.A., *Stafford Remembered* (1982), p.7

20   Hibbert, C., *A Handbook and Guide to Stafford* (1906)

21   SA, 20 July 1910

22   *Representation of the Mayor, Aldermen and Burgesses of Stafford to the Local Government Board as to the alteration of the boundary of the Borough* (1914), p.14

23   *Stafford: an Industrial Survey* (1932), p.12

24   Higson, p.9

25   Higson. Quotations in this and the following two paragraphs are all from this report.

Chapter Seven

1   *VCH*, vol. v, p.91

2   *VCH*, vol. v, p.92 and vol. vi, p.207

3   *VCH*, vol. vi, p.205

4   The grant is printed in full in Cherry, J.L., *Stafford in Olden Times* (1890), pp.121-5

5   LHSB L7, Lewis, R.A., *Stafford in 1600* (1971), p.27

6   LHSB L7, Lewis, R.A., *Stafford in 1600* (1971), p.29

7   Greenslade, M.W., *St Austin's, Stafford* (1991), p.5

8   Matthews, A.G., *Congregational Churches of Staffordshire* (1924), pp.34-6

9   Scammell, S.D., *Jubilee and Centenary of the Old Stafford Meeting House* (1887), pp.13-6

10   *Some Notes on the Society of Friends in Stafford* (1930), pp.1-7

11   Greenslade, M.W., *St Austin's, Stafford* (1991), pp.9-10

12   LHSB L39, Lewis, R.A., *Three Stafford Churches* (1980), pp.27-30

13   Quoted by Fisher, M.J., *A Vision of Splendour* (1995), p.39

14   Greenslade, M.W., 'Stafford in the 1851 Religious Census', *OSS*, (1974-6), pp.67-74

15   Roxburgh, pp.41-5

16   Roxburgh, pp.121-4

17   *VCH*, vol. vi, p.254 ; Roxburgh, pp.125-8

18   Fisher, M.J., *A Vision of Splendour* (1995), pp.32-64

19   The rest of this chapter is based on the following church histories: Anslow, J., *St Thomas's Church*, Stafford (1972); Fisher, M.J., *A Guide to St Mary's* (n.d.); Fisher, M.J. and Riley, M., *The Churches of St Bertelin in Stafford* (1981); Greenslade, M.W., *St Austin's, Stafford 1791-1991* (1991)—includes other Catholic churches; Imm, F., *St Paul's Forebridge* (1995)—includes St Peter's, Rickerscote; *Christ Church, Stafford* (1987)—includes Rowley Street Church; *Wesleyan Methodist Church, Stafford, Centenary Celebrations* (1964)

Chapter Eight

1   *VCH*, vol. vi, pp.164-5; Gilmore, C.G., *History of King Edward VI School, Stafford* (1953), chapter 2

2   Gilmore, C.G., *History of King Edward VI School, Stafford* (1953), pp.20-1

3   Bishop's Visitation, 1636, quoted in Johnson, D.A. and Vaisey, D.G., *Staffordshire and the Great Rebellion* (1964), p.11

4   For this and the following paragraphs see *VCH*, vol. vi, pp.164-7 and Gilmore, C.G., *History of King Edward VI School, Stafford* (1953)

5   Baker, *Wesleyan Sunday School, Stafford* (1905), pp.5-10

6   Greenslade, M.W., *St Austin's Stafford 1791-1991* (1991), pp.21-2

7   [Hawkins, T.], *Christ Church, Stafford* (1987)

8   Imm, F., *St Paul's Forebridge Past and Present* (1995), p.51

9   Collingwood, B.E., *John Wheeldon School*, SH&CS 1993, pp.12-4

10   Report of H.M. Inspector copied into *Log Book, Rowley Street School*, 1878

11   Gilmore, C.G., *History of King Edward VI School, Stafford* (1953) chapter 5

12   SA, 6 May 1870

13   SA, 17 December 1870; Salt, T., *Remarks on the Practical Application of the Elementary Education Act in Stafford* (1870)

14   Collingwood, B.E., *John Wheeldon School*, SH&CS 1993

15   *Log Book of Christ Church Girls' School*, 1896

16   Lewis, R.A., *Education in Staffordshire 1870-1970* p.19, WSL

17   Murcott, P., 'The Passive Resisters of Stafford', *SH&CS* 1965-7, pp.36-45

18   Balfour, G., *Ten Years of Staffordshire Education 1903-13* (1913), pp.126-7

19   Balfour, G., *Ten Years of Staffordshire Education 1903-13* (1913), pp.60-1

20   Lewis, R.A., *Education in Staffordshire 1870-1970*, pp.46-8, WSL

21   Names and dates of opening are in *VCH*, vol. vi, pp.263-4

Appendix

1   For the Stafford family before 1521 *see* Rawcliffe, C., *The Staffords, Earls of Stafford and Dukes of Buckingham* (1978)

2   LHSB L2, Lewis, R.A., *Stafford Castle* (revised 1983), pp.10-2

3   Salzman, L.F., *Building in England down to 1540* (1952), pp.438-9

4   Stitt, F.B., 'Stafford Borough Court Rolls 1396-7', *SH&CS* 1974-6, p.15

5   Compare names in *VCH* vol. vi, p.237, and Rawcliffe, C., *The Staffords, Earls of Stafford and Dukes of Buckingham* (1978)

6   Cherry, J.L., *Stafford in Olden Times* (1890), p.57

7   *Stafford Castle; Past Work and Recent Progress* (1984), p.27

8   de Mazzinghi, T.J., *Castlechurch*, SHC VIII (2), p.105

9   Langston, J.N., 'Old Catholic Families of Gloucestershire', *Transactions of the Bristol and Gloucestershire Archaeological Society*, vol. 72, pp.79-104, has an account of the Stafford family after 1521

10   Pennington, D.H. and Rootes, I.A., *The Committee at Stafford 1643-5*, SHC Fourth Series, vol. 1, p.21

11   SND, *Sir William Howard, Viscount Stafford* (1920) and Ireson, M., *Blessed William Howard* (1963)

12   Langston, J.N., 'The Jerninghams of Painswick', *Transactions of the Bristol and Gloucestershire Archaeological Society*, vol. 83, pp.114-8

13   LHSB L2, Lewis, R.A., *Stafford Castle* (revised 1983), pp.32-6 and 41 reprints the sources quoted

Index

References to illustrations are given in **bold**